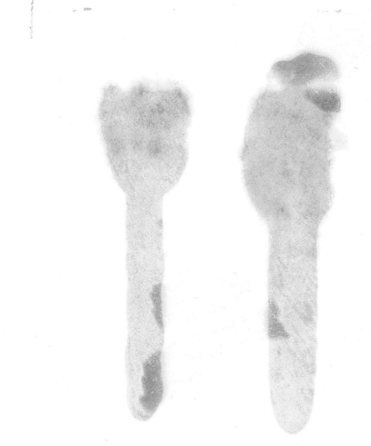

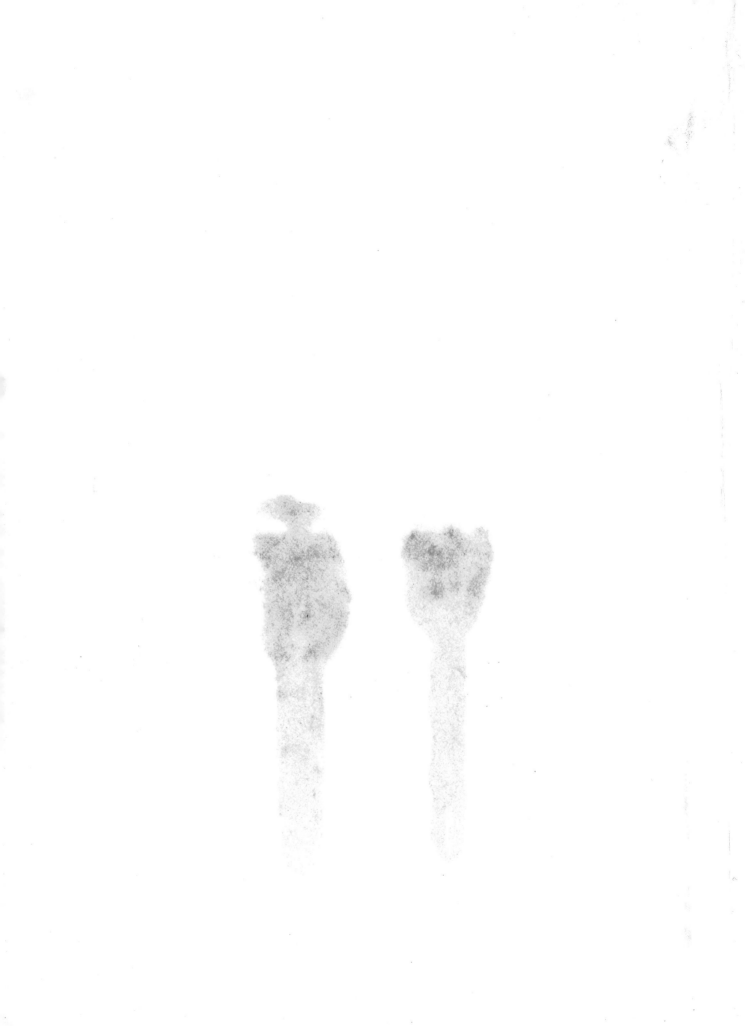

A PORTRAIT OF THE ITALIANS IN AMERICA

A PORTRAIT OF THE ITALIANS IN AMERICA

Vincenza Scarpaci

CHARLES SCRIBNER'S SONS • NEW YORK

*To those who accept the full drama of Italian
immigration: its beauty, blemishes, achievements,
and tragedies. May they better understand their
heritage through the view of life within these pages.
And to my family and friends who helped and
encouraged me to gather this record of
Italian life in America.*

Library of Congress Cataloging in Publication Data

Scarpaci, Vincenza.
A portrait of the Italians in America.

Includes bibliographical references and index.
I. Italian Americans—History—Pictorial works.
I. Title.

E184.18S27 1982   306'.089951073   82-10321
ISBN 0-684-16992-4

1 3 5 7 9 11 13 15 17 19   Q/C   20 18 16 14 12 10 8 6 4 2

Printed in the United States of America.

ACKNOWLEDGMENTS

While I must accept the full responsibility for and critical comments about the material in *A Portrait of the Italians in America*, I must also share any credit and praise with a long list of institutions and individuals. The humanity of the latter contributed in no small way to this book.

The archivists and photo librarians at the Library of Congress, the National Archives, the Urban Archives of Temple University and Wayne State University, the Minnesota Historical Society, and the staffs of the specialized depositories—the Hull House collection at the University of Illinois Circle Campus, the Balch Institute of Ethnic Studies, the Immigration History Research Center, the Multicultural History Society of Ontario, the Social Ethics Collection at Harvard University, the Smithsonian Institution, and the Merrimack Textile Museum—not only helped to guide me to photo sources, but also expressed a genuine interest and support in my project.

Those official sources of materials provided the foundation for me to develop a basic framework and outline. But the personal magic that added life and warmth to these pages belongs to my friends and colleagues, who went beyond the rules of academic cooperation to seek out materials for me and to share the information and photos they had accumulated in their own research. My colleagues Phylis Martinelli, George Pozzetta, Gary Mormino, Archie Motley, Philip Notarianni, Luciano Iorizzo, Carlo Ferroni, Anthony Pizzo, William D'Antonio, Thora Jacobsen, Walter Rosenblaum, and Alessandro Baccari belong to a special category.

Then there is a long list of people who offered their help and suggestions or responded enthusiastically to my requests. Dorothy Mullen Marcucci encouraged me to send out notices to Italian-American newspapers and *IAM* magazine describing my project and asking for materials. The response was amazing. Italian Americans sent cherished family photos to me, a person they had never met but who had asked for their help in telling the story of Italians in America. Some of their pictures appear in these pages, and their names are given in the Picture Credits section. I want to thank personally as many of them as possible: Nicholas Sammartino, Arturo Mazziotti, Gerald Sbarbaro, Ioli Giomi, Anita Pietromartire, Dom Accetta, George Pasadore, Rachel Becchetti Verretto, and Helen Becchetti Dover. My friend George Samos copied the pictures I received in the mail.

My friend Julia Santini in Detroit supplied me with a treasure of family photos. Zena Valenziano, Joseph Dell'Alba, Anthony and Ann Sorentino, Jo Ann Pilardi Fuchs, Ann Rinaldi, Joseph and Vincenza Amato, Anthony Codianni, Frank and Sarah Giordano, Sam Longo, and Philip Cosentino also checked through family albums for me. Ace Alagna of the *Italian Tribune News* of Newark shared his collection of successful and well-known Italian Americans.

Just as Mario Puzo admitted at the height of his national acclaim that his family, and especially his mother, provided the personal Italian-American flavor in his novel *The Fortunate Pilgrim*, I, too, find these evidences in this book. My family (the Gerardis, Gentiles, and Scarpacis) provided the usual support and comfort all authors require during the long process of creating a book. My family also contributed pictures and asked their friends for additional ones. And while everyone expects the author to praise his or her family, few authors have the privilege I have of thanking my Italian-American mother for helping to type the captions and text while being constant in her belief that our efforts would help to commemorate the immigrant experience of which she is so proud.

CONTENTS

PREFACE

The vivid image of the growth of a nation and the life of its people challenges those who attempt to document it. The picture, a visual record of a moment in time, lends credibility because it illustrates history. Its literalness suggests objectivity. Each photograph gains value as the viewer's attention focuses on its detail, accepting it as an accurate portrayal of the scene. Each photo sets an example of the moment described as if it were typical for all such moments.

The pictures in *A Portrait of the Italians in America* only suggest the story of Italians in America. They are not the complete story of a people—only fleeting glimpses of their experience. But they do offer an opportunity to see the physical, human, and sometimes psychic landscape of the immigrants' new world.

With all their limitations, however, photographs allow a visual interpretation of reality. The pictures here help us to imagine other times and places: the crowded streets of Naples, the press of humanity in crowded ships bound for America, the substandard working and living conditions, and the contrast of traditional clothing and customs in a new environment.

These fleeting glimpses depict the variety of life in North America as experienced by the Italian immigrant; they help to highlight the fact that the Italian migration touched every area of American life, every region of the American continent. From the early explorers to the pioneering prelates, from the individual adventurers and refugees to the many Italians who arrived at the turn of the century, this movement covered a broad cross section of the Italian population and it offered a variety of skills, cultural gifts, and strong backs to the New World. The collection of photos in *A Portrait of the Italians in America*, then, addresses the multicolored and multifaceted experience that has so influenced the lives of the people of America.

INTRODUCTION

The Italian imprint on North America began with the voyages of Christopher Columbus, John Cabot, Amerigo Vespucci, and Giovanni da Verrazzano and continued through the European settlement, when Italian Jesuits and itinerant craftsmen traveled to the New World for God, adventure, freedom, and economic necessity.

With the support of the Spanish, Columbus opened up new areas for European expansion. That land, sighted in 1492, was later named after the Italian navigator Vespucci. In 1499 Vespucci and Alonso de Ojeda named the land they saw along the northern end of South America "Venezuela," or "little Venice" in Florentine dialect. Vespucci's accounts of his voyages prompted a German cartographer, Martin Waldseemüller, to name the land mass to the south of the Caribbean "America." (A 1511 map by Gerhardus Mercator, a Flemish geographer, extended this name to the northern part of the continent.) The Venetian John Cabot (born Giovanni Caboto) sighted Newfoundland and claimed it for King Henry VII of England. In 1524 Verrazzano, sailing for Francis I of France, was the first European to voyage up the east coast from North Carolina past Cape Cod to Newfoundland. His descriptions of New York harbor, his account of the native American population, and encouraging reports about the agricultural potential of the land along the coast whetted the appetite of those seeking colonial riches.

During the sixteenth and seventeenth centuries, European expeditions and settlement projects included Italian priests and attracted immigrants with special skills. Italians in the Spanish Jesuit order traveled across the continent, establishing missions in the southwest, north central, and northwestern regions. In 1539 Marcos de Niza, a Franciscan missionary, explored Arizona and New Mexico for Spain, and communicated with the Zuni and Pima. Between 1687 and 1711 an Italian Jesuit, Eusebio Kino, traveled throughout Mexico, Arizona, and California, mapping the land, establishing missions, and introducing European crops and the practice of raising cattle.

Another Italian Jesuit, Gregorio Mengarini, worked in 1841 with the Indians in part of the northwestern territory that was to become Montana. He not only ministered to the Indians, but rendered their language, Salish, into *A Salish or Flat Head Grammar* in 1861.

Henry de Tonti, a soldier born in Gaeta, Italy, accompanied the French Canadian government expedition in 1679 and braved the dangers

of the wilderness to travel westward across the Great Lakes and then journeyed with Robert Cavelier, Sieur de La Salle, down the length of the
mighty Mississippi. (Tonti and La Salle erected a column at the mouth of
the Mississippi River in 1682, claiming the territory for France.)

A sprinkling of Italian craftsmen also crossed the Atlantic in the seventeenth century to take advantage of the demand for skilled workers.
Many were invited, such as the Italian glassblowers who settled in James-
town. Early Italian arrivals paralleled the story of the Pilgrims. In 1657 a
group of Italian Protestants, the Waldenses, left the Piedmont region and
arrived in New Amsterdam. They sought refuge from religious persecution
in the settlement they established at New Castle, Delaware. One hundred
Italian indentured servants were brought in 1768 to raise indigo plants in
New Smyrna, Florida. In the years before the American Revolution, Philip
Mazzei, a friend of Thomas Jefferson and Benjamin Franklin, offered his
political ideas and European plants and agriculture to the nation's
founders.

In the early records of the English colonies, there are traces of Italian
musicians, figure carvers, language teachers, wine merchants, and distinguished visitors. For example, Giovanni Gualdo, a wine merchant as well
as a composer and conductor, arrived in Philadelphia via London in 1767.
The Milanese botanist Count Luigi Castiglioni traveled through the new
nation between 1785 and 1787, and his observations on the thirteen
states, the national government, the Constitution, and, of course, the in-
teresting plants he saw were published in 1790. Lorenzo Da Ponte, Mo-
zart's librettist, came to New York from Venice in 1805 and taught Italian
and Italian literature at Columbia University. Pietro Bacchi, a Sicilian
scholar exiled for his revolutionary political activities, accepted a teaching
position in Spanish and Italian at Harvard College.

Italian sculptors, such as Giuseppe Ceracchi, traveled and worked in
the new nation during the 1790s. Ceracchi executed portrait busts of
George Washington and John Adams, and, while in Philadelphia, tutored
American sculptor William Rush. Other Italian sculptors who came to
America were Giovanni Andrei and Giuseppe Franzoni. They came at the
invitation of Thomas Jefferson to do work on the Capitol. Earlier, Jefferson
had employed Italian marble cutters to build the University of Virginia
and was responsible for recruiting fourteen Italian musicians to form the
first marine band.

Italian opera, opera houses built especially for Italian opera, and Ital-
ian singers became part of the early cultural life of urban America. Gio-
vanni Grassi, an Italian Jesuit, became president of Georgetown
University; Giovanni Nobili and Michael Accolti established Santa Clara
College in California; Joseph Cataldo, after an active life spent in Montana,
Idaho, Wyoming, Oregon, Alaska, and Washington (1867–1928), founded
Gonzaga University in Spokane, Washington.

Records from the colonial period are scanty, and each state government handled its own immigration records. It was not until 1820 that the
federal government began recording its own statistics, but even then, it
was difficult to maintain accuracy because of the multipolitical units of a

disunited, diverse Italy. Between 1820 and 1865, approximately 17,000 Italians entered North America. They settled mainly along the East Coast but some went west, literally opening the way for future generations. Italian seamen reached the West Coast in the 1830s, and the lure of gold attracted a larger number in 1849. Most were from Genoa, and their government, the Kingdom of Sardinia, sent a consul in 1850, Colonel Leonetto Cipriani, to San Francisco. In 1822 Giacomo Constantino Beltrami explored Minnesota, looking for the headwaters of the Mississippi River. Businessmen, such as Francesco Grossi, were selling ice cream in Toronto, Canada, in the 1830s. And in 1862 John Owen Dominis, the son of an Italian-American sea captain from Boston who had settled in Hawaii in 1819, married Queen Liliuokalani, the last reigning monarch of that nation before it was annexed to the United States.

These early pioneers established a link to Italy that reflected the economic culture of Italy and the political turmoil of a divided nation. As North American cities flourished, the tastes of the citizenry dwelt on the fashions, designs, architecture, and art forms of Europe. A look at the census of most early nineteenth-century North American cities shows Italian hairdressers, figure makers, language and music teachers, marble carvers, ship chandlers, and purveyors of fancy imported goods. Their major motivation for emigrating was the lure of economic opportunity, but some were political fugitives exiled because of their participation in organizations outlawed by the reigning princes or because of the failed revolutions of 1830 and 1848.

Yet, even this early outpouring of Italian migration loses significance against the larger pageant of population movement. For centuries, Italian seamen, explorers, merchants, and workers had traveled as far as China and as close as North Africa. When Columbus set forth on his voyages, colonies of Italians were living in Lisbon, Seville, Marseilles, and Constantinople. Even the early explorers labored for foreign monarchs just as did the Italian craftsmen who traveled to the swamplands along the Baltic and transformed the area into the glittering St. Petersburg during the reign of Peter the Great.

It was the combination of the Risorgimento (unification), the transformation of Italian industry and agricultural organization of the mid-nineteenth century, and overpopulation that sent thousands of Italians away from their homes. Outside Italy the availability of cheap transportation, recruitment, and incentives offered by foreign governments and the invisible hand of capitalism combined to match those in search of work with those in need of workers.

Large-scale emigration from Italy began in the early nineteenth century from the north. Immigrants traveled from Lombardy, Emilia-Romagna, and Venetia to South America, Argentina and Brazil especially, but also to Uruguay, which used government subsidies to encourage settlement, mainly for agricultural colonies. Italian workers from northern Italy had traveled on a seasonal basis to jobs in France, Switzerland, Germany, and even Tunis, but some later switched from this seasonal movement to take advantage of the inverted climate of South America—picking crops there during the Italian winter. Italian involvement in Latin American life ran the gamut from the role of Giuseppe Garibaldi in fighting for the liberation of Uruguay to the cosmopolitan cities of Sao Paolo and Buenos Aires, whose populations were predominantly Italian. Italian immigrants made up nearly half of all arrivals in Brazil and they were the largest group of foreigners in Argentina. Compared to this infiltration of Italians into Latin America, the larger number of immigrants in North America—over 4 million who arrived between 1820 and 1920—takes on a different perspective. In North America the immigrant population remained a small percentage of the native born. Unlike Argentina, where a public election was held to determine whether the official language of the country should be Spanish or Italian, North America maintained the customs and traditions of the Anglo-Saxon language. Of course, during times of economic uncertainty and social unrest, the establishment believed itself in a state of siege as thousands of foreigners entered. Their numbers, however, did not translate into the power needed to challenge the social order; in fact, most wished to join that order, not to change it.

The unification of Italy in 1861 tipped the emigrant balance from north to south. Laws prohibiting emigration had been strictly enforced in the Kingdom of the Two Sicilies. The easing of restrictions, coupled with such factors as population growth, insufficient and ill-used land resources, inadequate economic development, as well as individual motives, accelerated the exodus.

While unification had accompanied industrial development in the north, the Piedmontese rulers did not extend their economic program into the south. The freeing of Italians from foreign domination and local oppression did not signal the end of inequities or injustice. The large latifundi owned by the church and foreign nobility merely changed hands. Italy's entry into the world of industrial manufacture led to competition with other European countries. Tariffs acted as barriers to reduce outside competition, and yet they were not limited to manufactured goods, but also placed on agricultural exports—a mainstay of the south's economy. Unification also introduced a more efficient internal tax system that exacted revenues from all regions, but did not share these revenues on an equitable basis. Therefore, the tax system further drained the resources of the south.

As conditions in the south contributed to an outward population flow, again the destinations varied. While the majority of emigrants headed across the Atlantic Ocean, some settled in South America. Others traveled to Australia, North Africa, and other parts of Europe. This southern explosion did not signal an end to emigration from northern Italy. Emigrants still left, but in smaller numbers.

As the momentum for migration increased, other factors were at work directing Italians to North America. Improvements in transatlantic transportation, a result of technological progress, and the growth of trade between North America and Europe also played an important role. By the 1870s steamships crossed the Atlantic in ten days. Trade routes that linked American ports with Europe became conduits for human traffic.

The Italian ports of Genoa, Naples, and later Trieste and Palermo featured dramatic departure scenes daily. The emigration business employed more than 10,000 in Italy. Ticket agents, boardinghouses, dockside hucksters, draymen, recruitment agents, manifesto printers, as well as stevedores, food and ship suppliers, seamen, government inspectors, and port officials represented an expanding industry.

The turning point for Italian immigration to America was 1880. While some 70,000 came to North America between 1866 and 1879, close to 4 million arrived between 1880 and 1914. The high point of Italian immigration to America occurred between 1900 and 1910, when more than 2 million entered. Most entered through the port of New York—97 percent of those arriving in 1900 entered via Ellis Island, and of those Italians who arrived in Boston, Philadelphia, and New Orleans, 54 percent gave New York as their destination. Of course, not all immigrants remained in New York City. At least two-thirds of the Italians bound for Canada also arrived in New York. New York, like Naples, developed an industry designed to provide the accommodations and services necessary to expedite this human traffic. Men, women, and children paused there en route to the hinterland to join family or work crews in mines and factories. In 1907 alone, as many as 285,000 Italians arrived in America.

Official statistics can do no more than suggest the implications of such a population movement. They paint a broad stroke across the canvas of history without acknowledging the variety it encompasses. For example, the official count was inaccurate. Before the unification of Italy, many Italians lived under foreign governments. Some emigrated first to other European countries, then to America and were listed under those jurisdictions. Some entered illegally. Many returned to Italy either on a seasonal basis or permanently—estimates range as high as one-third.

Migration chains developed in many ways. Men between the ages of fourteen and forty-five made up the bulk of the late nineteenth-century migration. They were recruited to work in mines, on railroads, in factories, and they were directed to locales by steamship agents, *paesani* who wished to enlarge their commercial investments. Many towns in North America were so much alike that newcomers, with a limited knowledge of geography, had a hazy view of the nation in which they would eventually build their homes. Yet, they were somehow able to describe a neighborhood in the North End of Boston or one in Pueblo, Colorado.

The majority of immigrants were agrarian. In America they transferred *la zappa,* or "the hoe," to the pick-and-shovel work required to build the communication infrastructure. The Italian contribution to the refining of America also derives from the immigrant labor used to build reservoirs, streetcar lines, subways, railroads, and buildings, to pave streets, and to install and repair sewage lines.

While the unskilled immigrant contributed his strength and his labor, the skilled artisans—stonecutters, masons, bricklayers, tailors, carpenters—and horticulturists provided experience and skill. When expert building craftsmen were required, North America looked to Italian artisans to do the ornate marble decorations on its public buildings, such as the

South Carolina State House, and the mosaic tile grandeur of the indoor Roman pool at William Randolph Hearst's castle at San Simeon, California.

The immigrant population also clustered in the industrial Northeast, where the combination of jobs and established colonies offered a semblance of *ambiente*. However, across the continent smaller circles of settlement developed, many by chance, such as the people from Carunchio who settled the community of White Cloud in northeastern Kansas. Robert Severo described the settlement in America of his ancestors as follows: "Always, I was told, they went because they had a friend—but surely there was somebody at one point who went and who had no friend."

However small in number, Italian immigrants established their presence. Wherever they settled—in cities or towns—the Italians' custom of intensive agriculture to provide for their own family and for local markets expanded the truck-farming industry and introduced new vegetables to the American table. *Contadini* skills at raising and marketing fruits and vegetables created a renaissance in the wholesale and retail trades. Produce market areas from Baltimore and New Orleans to Detroit, Kansas City, and Seattle were dominated by the immigrant entrepreneur.

Italian immigrants in search of work or adventure fanned out across this country. Before California became part of the United States, Italian seamen and merchants braved the sea voyage around Cape Horn and visited the small Spanish settlements. The discovery of gold in 1849 accelerated this influx. Throughout the world Italian seamen were part of the harbor life. Their services centered on transporting goods from one port to another. They shipped coal from Wales, marble to Baltimore, wine from France. Each American port city experienced this transient Italian traffic. Over time, some Italian immigrants who read or heard about opportunities in the American West traveled directly to places like Albuquerque, New Mexico. Most of this fanning out resulted from the location of work. Labor agents, operating in Chiasso in Switzerland, New York, Chicago, Montreal, and in small mining, railroad, and factory towns across North America, channeled this human stream to work sites. Agents linked job seekers with employers. Federal and state governments and private entrepreneurs advertised, encouraged, and even paid fees to acquire a labor force. Many men from Italy arrived in port cities with tags attached to their clothes, indicating their North American destination, the place where they would work.

For some immigrants, the work experience resulted in settlement. It was usually the combination of work location, living costs, and the need to be among *paesani,* and a response to the indifference or hostility of the American population, that fostered the growth of Little Italies. Concentrations of Italian population enabled the development and growth of ethnic business: Butchers kept goats for Easter; grocers imported olive oil from the region favored by their clientele; saloons sold beer and wine and provided tables for Italian card games; and boardinghouses often expanded into simple *casalingo* restaurants, offering Italian dishes.

In some locales *paese,* or family, identification was reflected in housing patterns. Calabrese lived on one street, Neapolitans on the next. In some cases, all the apartments in a building were rented out to relatives and their friends. Many boarding arrangements developed in a similar fashion. Apartments and houses were fashioned to resemble those of far distant *paese*. While social aspects of immigrant life began at the basic level of food and shelter, it then moved into the areas of religion, business, work, and recreation.

Although the Italians brought with them an attachment to the *paese* world they left behind, they were able to adjust to the different forms it took in America. Grocery store owners, insurance salesmen, and barbers learned the dialects of their patrons; membership in recreational clubs and church organizations crossed *paese* lines; inter-*paese* and regional ties grew as children attended the same schools; women shopped at the same stores; and adults worked together and enjoyed each other's company as they spent warm summer evenings together. The larger world of the Italian immigrants did not erase their primary *paese* identity, but rather expanded it to include the new world in which they found themselves.

For most immigrants, life *oltremare,* or beyond the sea, was harsh and unpredictable. The predominantly male sojourners traveled to America to earn money, then return home. Those with skills could choose a locale and turn their talents into a comfortable living. But many artisans found that the American industrial system placed them in a controlled economic setting. For example, a shoemaker from Bari ran a machine in a Lynn, Massachusetts, factory and his skill earned him more than the untrained workers, but he had little claim to the social status he had enjoyed in Italy. The tailor joined the ranks of the garment industry, where clothes were mass-produced. Only a few could seek the quality custom tailoring that catered to the upper classes. Produce merchants, food importers, and truck farmers began in modest, marginal ways, going from door to door, selling goods at prices their American competitors disdained, seeking new products, and facing the challenge of marginality. For some, success echoed that of Horatio Alger. Immigrants who owned produce stores went into wholesale merchandising; those who were hucksters opened freight hauling businesses; and those involved in marginal truck farming developed strawberry cooperatives. The majority of the immigrants earned modest incomes with long hours and family assistance. Pushcart peddlers ripened bananas in their cellars, and the children of the iceman rose at five in the morning to help load their father's wagon.

The pick-and-shovel men traveled to shape-ups at construction sites in Baltimore the same way day laborers congregated in the town piazza in Italy. Others sought the help of fellow townsmen or labor bosses who supplied railroad companies, mine companies, and factories with workers. The difficulty of not knowing English made the *padrone* middleman (sometimes also banker, letter writer, ticket agent, saloon or boardinghouse keeper) an important link in the immigrant chain.

Immigrants laboring in the slate quarries of eastern Pennsylvania, the smelting industries at Meaderville, Montana, and Pueblo, Colorado, the mines in southern Illinois and Jerome, Arizona, also suffered from loneliness, exploitation, and bone-tiring, dangerous work.

The women who emigrated with their families or to join husbands found employment near their homes. Depending on the location and the availability of work, Italian women contributed to their family income. Although in some regions in Italy work for women was restricted to the home, to the immediate family, or *paese*-supervised occupations, such as the silk workers of Lombardy and the women farm laborers in Apulia, in North America the economy based on cash forced many to enter the work force. In Buffalo, New York, women worked in the canneries outside the city; throughout the truck-farming areas across America they helped harvest crops; in Providence, Rhode Island, they worked in factories or at home making jewelry; in Chicago women shelled and sorted nuts, made candy, worked in the men's clothing industry; in New York City women made artificial flowers and children's toys and finished clothing at home or in factory lofts; and in Tampa, Florida, Italian women worked in the cigar industry. Most often they helped their entrepreneur husband. One Baltimore woman helped her husband push and pull a hurdy-gurdy to the fair in Gettysburg, Pennsylvania (seventy miles), each year. Other women did the same volume of work as their husbands did in grocery stores, butcher shops, bakeries, and restaurants.

Children, too, were part of this economic enterprise. In Italy compulsory education, when established and enforced, provided three years of rudimentary instruction. Many immigrants were semiliterate. The rate of illiteracy for women was higher, since education was considered an unnecessary luxury for most. In America, much of this traditional attitude continued. Most children left school as early as the law allowed so that they could begin work. Parents were caught between the lure of free education and the economic necessities of life. Some chose the former, making many sacrifices to help their children to further their education. Some took advantage of evening schools, while others helped in their family business while they attended high school and college.

This harsh life, far removed from a familiar landscape and family surroundings, heightened the tensions of daily work. The emerging industrial giants treated labor as another cost in production. They paid the lowest wages they could and usually preferred quantity to quality, which allowed them to dismiss workers who questioned long hours, low pay, and unsafe working conditions. However, mutual-assistance organizations developed at many work sites. They provided benefits for widows and orphans, funeral arrangements, and some aid for those who became sick or injured. Some of these societies reflected the occupations of their members. For example, San Francisco, California, and Gloucester, Massachusetts, had one for fishermen and Baltimore, Maryland, had one for tailors. Others reflected the *paese* or region of Italy, such as the Contessa Entellina Society of New Orleans, the Matrice Club of Cleveland, or the Lega Toscana of New York. These groups offered social activities for their members, ranging from shore parties along the Chesapeake Bay favored by Baltimore's Italians to the annual August picnic of the Dante Alighieri Society in the Sunrise-Hartville area of Wyoming. These societies helped to make the transition to life in America much easier for the Italian immigrant.

One of the characteristics most noted about Italian immigration was the predominance of males. Essentially, the movement to North America simply extended the seasonal economic pattern long established by workers traveling all over Europe. Those men who left alone, with a relative, or in a group of *paesani* sought employment as a way to maintain their well being. The wages they earned were sent back or brought back to the *paese.* Their voyage, however far, still bound them to the community they left behind. The transition from sojourner to settler was a subtle one. The choice to move to America was not always a conscious decision, merely the acceptance that the wages earned in North America shored up the dependent family in the *paese.* Sojourners traveled back and forth fully expecting to return permanently to the *paese.* The process varied. Some fathers introduced their sons to the commuting arrangement; brothers, cousins, uncles, *paesani* did the same. In this way, the American experience was shared and assumed a communal aspect. The process extended to sisters, wives, and mothers when the family reassembled in North America. Some immigrants acknowledged that they felt more than an economic tie to North America. They responded to the variety of work opportunities and the promise of future advancement for their children.

But the decision to leave Italy was never simple. Many families never reunited. Some families were abandoned or forgotten. Individual immigrants experienced difficulties adjusting to the cultural crossing, unable to reconcile the differences and feeling uncomfortable and insecure. They longed for the familiar that was lost and were repelled by the strangeness of their new environment. Most accounts of immigration, however, stress the positive aspects: the valiant struggle, the brief reverses, then the long-sought-after victory—the purchase of a house, the economic security of steady work, the achievements of the children. The stories brush past the reality of daily marginality, the sense of loss, the uncertainty of one's choice, the fear of discrimination and hostility, the frustration of not having the choice to go back, the alienation from other family members (usually American-born children) and *paesani* who appeared to repudiate all attachment to the language and customs in order to gain acceptance as Americans.

Some immigrants cushioned the adjustment cycle by encapsulating themselves within their re-created *paese* environment. In the large Italian-American settlements, entire sections seemed to resemble Naples more than the New World. The Little Italies of North America provided for some a cultural continuity, and within these locales, the concentration of immigrants supported a way of life that maintained a cultural, economic, and social identity. Spoken Italian and dialects filled the streets; familiar smells of cheese, salami, and garlic wafted on the breeze; street music was provided by the hurdy gurdy and the organ grinder; women compared produce bought from a huckster's cart; and posters announced Italian theater and opera performances or proclaimed the street entertainment of the puppet shows. While the majority of the citizens in the Little Italies of North America lived in the crowded substandard housing abandoned by the native Americans—usually in the oldest sections of the cities—their social structure reflected a cross-section of the immigrant population. The successful professional might not actually live there, but he maintained his office in the area; the businessmen, bankers, merchants, skilled craftsmen, and day laborers recreated a holistic community. Large numbers of people sometimes led to the establishment and maintenance of Italian churches served by Italian clergy.

Even in some rural areas and small towns, such as St. Helena, North Carolina; Tontitown, Arkansas; Newburgh, New York; and Wood River, Illinois, an Italian population introduced the character of *ambiente* in a limited but spirited way, from the celebration of a patron saint's day to the introduction of new crops, intensive agriculture, and *paesani* fraternity. While to some native Americans the Little Italies appeared to be re-creations of the Old World towns, this was not true. First, some non-Italians lived in every Little Italy; second, each immigrant concentration contained people from different *paese, citta, regione,* and *provincia;* and third, distinctions were made within the community according to how long one had been in North America. (Those who had arrived earlier often appeared American to the newly arrived imigrants.) Therefore, the multifaceted nature of Italian-American life prevented homogeneity. Institutionalized ethnicity promoted by fraternal organizations, religious activities, and the establishment of social agencies, such as hospitals, orphanages, schools, sports clubs, and immigrant aid societies, provided a veneer to cover the layered composite underneath.

Most important, everything Italian that distinguished the immigrant from the native—language, food, dress, traditions, religion, and values—could not remain immune to the surrounding culture. North America's mass-produced and inexpensive clothing, furniture, and household items influenced individuals, but while the pots and pans in every home might be standard items, the ever-present cheese grater, colander, pizzelle iron, or *gitarra* reflected Old World continuity.

The Italian immigrant who attended mass and participated in church activities discovered that Roman Catholicism in America reflected the religious traditions of the Irish Catholics, who dominated the hierarchy. The religious expression and form of worship followed by the Italian immigrant appeared flamboyant, excessive, and pagan to other Roman Catholics. Street parades in which the saint's statue was carried on the shoulders of the crowd and money offerings were pinned to the statue's garments, bands played stirring dramatic music, and vendors cooked and sold food and drink shocked the sensibilities of a clergy who believed that dignity and respect required restrained and orderly devotion, with the priest guiding the faithful in demeanor as well as worship.

Naturally, Italian immigrants did not feel welcome in this atmosphere. The newcomers could hear their masses in Italian but they were often forced to attend them in church basements. Even those American-born clergymen sensitive to the problems of the newcomers had mixed feelings about separate services conducted in foreign languages by foreign priests. They preferred to encourage rapid assimilation through the process of religion. Their reluctant acceptance of national (nationality-oriented) parish churches was based on the assumption that the Americanization of the second and third generations would soon end the linguistic and cultural differences between Catholics. Outside the national parishes, some neighborhood parishes requested the assignment of an assistant pastor of Italian background to conduct special services on the days of their favorite saints. Special orders of Italian religious men and women were formed to minister to the spiritual needs of the immigrants. The Salesians, Scalabrini, Sisters of the Sacred Heart, and the Filippini were the most prominent.

For many Italian men, particularly for the southern Italians, the church, both in Italy and America, filled few worldly needs. Most men attended church only on special occasions, such as to serve as a godparent or to get married. In southern Italy the church had controlled vast estates on which the *contadini* labored, and even though the local clergy dispensed no charity, they expected donations or in-kind payment for every service rendered. The resentment against this situation in Italy did not lessen in America, where the clergy also expected the congregation to support the expenses of the parish. Men who sacrificed simple comforts to send money to families in Italy rejected the notion of weekly contributions to the church.

The hostility toward the organized church and a low rate of church attendance did not mean that the immigrant lacked religious devotion. Individually, the majority of men, as well as women, considered themselves Christians. They expressed their faith in their own manner, especially during feast day celebrations, by fasting or by lighting devotional candles in church or at home.

In America, Protestant missionaries interpreted Italian religious behavior as a sign of disinterest in Catholicism. Believing the immigrant sections ripe for proselytizing efforts, they established missions, day schools, and health services in the Little Italies. Their staffs of volunteers reflected the middle class—sincerely religious and dedicated native American women who wished to bring both orderliness and spiritual comfort to the immigrant. The missions served milk and cookies, and sometimes meals to the children who attended. They offered classes in child care, sewing, English, music, and the Bible. Whether Methodist, Presbyterian, Baptist, or Episcopal, the missions attempted to obtain Italian pastors or men who spoke Italian for this work. Italian immigrant pastors joined their North American brethren in ministering to the immigrant population, offering social services as well as spiritual guidance. For the most part, they seemed to teach by example—to dispense Christian charity and help without exacting payment or the promise of conversion. In each of the major cities, small Protestant congregations were formed, consisting of immigrants grateful for the personal care provided by the missions and interested in a religion that stressed the participation and understanding of the laity. Although many second-generation Italians remember receiving financial aid (clothes or shoes), attending play school, or enjoying cookies and milk in the Protestant mission, they accepted the aid without adopting the religion. Those few immigrants who did convert formed loyal and dedicated congregations.

Although Roman Catholicism was the established faith of the Italian nation, and most immigrants felt some allegiance toward it, not every Italian identified with its teachings. A small group of political radicals, anarchists, communists, and many socialists condemned organized religion as a form of exploitation. In North America these anticlerics would speak out against church activity when it seemed to dull political consciousness. A priest who counseled his flock not to strike or join a union would set the political critics into action.

Few Italian Jews emigrated to North America until the late 1930s, when Hitler's anti-Semitism was extended into Italy by Benito Mussolini. Prominent Italians, such as Enrico Fermi and Arturo Toscanini, whose wives were Jewish, and Emilio Segrè found refuge in the United States.

Wherever Italians settled, but especially in the Little Italies of North America, Old World traits were transplanted into the new soil. The maintenance of these customs varied according to the different environments, and adaptations and mutations resulted. Italian street vendors sold chestnuts and clams and produce from boxes strapped to their shoulders or pushcarts or wagons. Open-air markets operated daily in crowded immigrant sections. Women shopped every day, seeking bargains and arguing about the prices of items in a way reminiscent of the Old World, but in North America, they would buy items missing from *paese* markets, such as bananas and inexpensive, mass-produced clothing and shoes. And their preference for cheeses, olive oil, canned tomatoes, and macaroni in turn created opportunities for Italian importers and distributors. Salesmen representing import houses traveled to Italian communities where they supplied family groceries with the products wanted by the customers. *Padrone* or individual entrepreneurs often followed work crews to railroad construction sites, where they established commissaries. A Baltimore man operated such a business for Italian miners in Kaiser, West Virginia; an immigrant in Donaldsonville, Louisiana, drove his wagon from sugar plantation to sugar plantation selling Italian products to the immigrant cane workers.

Whenever possible, immigrants from the land continued to raise or make the foodstuffs they preferred. In urban backyards and open lots and along railroads tracks, Italians raised whatever fruit and vegetables the climate would support. Some built brick ovens in their backyards to bake bread, or they took their homemade dough to the ovens of the local bakers. Many women made their macaroni at home. Before the holidays merchants might order special items to be shipped directly from Naples or Genoa or through New York, Philadelphia, or Boston. Some immigrants asked relatives or *paesani* still in Italy to send crates of lemons, cheeses, olive oil, and figs. At holiday time native American farmers found customers for their goats and lambs in the immigrant neighborhoods.

Daily life for the typical immigrant family centered around the home, whether it was a tenement apartment or a modest one-family house. Coffee and milk with hard bread or toasted bread were served for breakfast to children and adults. Since the working men left early, their wives awakened at five o'clock to purchase cold cuts for the sandwiches their men would eat at work. Children also rose early to help with chores, such as lighting the furnace, loading their father's wagon, or delivering the bread he baked. Those women who stayed up late every night finishing clothes, making paper flowers, decorating hats, making lace, and so on faced a full day of routine household duties. Washing clothes and sheets for a family of five by hand could take an entire day. Many tasks were interrupted as the day progressed, such as when the children returned from school for lunch, for a trip to shop for dinner, or for the preparation of dinner.

Many children worked after school, helping merchants load carts, collecting rags and newspapers for sale, or helping in the family business. One second-generation man whose father ran a butcher shop said that at age sixteen his father would leave the entire operation of the shop in his hands. Some families depended strongly on the few pennies their children earned, and one immigrant son remembers how his mother waited each night for him to bring the pennies he earned from his paper route so she could shop for the family dinner. Children also helped their mothers with work at home—finishing clothes, making flowers, and so on. They threaded needles, removed bastings, sewed buttons, and picked up and delivered bundles of clothing to the contract shops in the neighborhood.

Recreational choices were governed by income and work schedules. Most North American workers labored six days a week, usually ten hours a day. Most evenings were spent resting from the day's toil. In the summer, visiting with neighbors on stoops, steps, porches, or park benches was the basic form of socialization. Relatives and *paesani* visited each other on Sundays or dropped in for a glass of wine or coffee during the week. Also on Sundays families often took streetcars to the nearest park or recreational area to eat outdoors. Urban families also went on excursions to the country to pick cardone, ciccora, and blackberries. Men played cards and drank wine, and some immigrants joined their friends in the neighborhood saloon. Women often mended clothes, crocheted, and chatted. At the immigrant theaters, Italians could hear Shakespeare in Italian or a variety show featuring the character comedian Farfariello, whose sketches reflected immigrant life. In the large cities, Italian opera was part of the cultural life, and Italian immigrants purchased family circle tickets to cheer their favorite singers, and many Italian opera stars, conductors, and musicians toured North America.

Those immigrants who belonged to mutual benefit, *paese,* or fraternal associations attended monthly meetings and social events. The death of an association's member meant attendance by all at the funeral. These groups also joined in the celebration of Columbus Day or, in some areas, Pioneer Days. They wore their organizational regalia—usually sashes in green, white, and red with the emblem of their society—as they marched behind the bands, which were made up of professional and amateur musicians, including Italian immigrants, and which played operatic airs and marches.

Throughout the nineteenth century, the predominant social theory in America concerned the melting pot, and such institutions as the church and school hoped to hasten the transition from Italian immigrant to American. Starting at Ellis Island (or Castle Garden, New York's immigration reception station before Ellis Island), the immigrant began to incorporate American ideals, customs, clothes, and language, which led to a unique culture, one that used the contributions of the immigrants to create a new system. Hidden somewhere in the American culture were the bits and pieces taken from the European immigrants. The American culture homogenized these components so that no one of its parts could be identified as foreign. In public school Italian children, like their Czech, German, Greek, or Finnish schoolmates, were encouraged by word as well as example to give up the traditions of their parents. It was stressed that American ways, from hygiene to history, were better, and native American classmates, unaccustomed to the ways of other groups, expressed their ignorance through ridicule. Immigrant children were embarrassed by the differences and most came to believe that their parents were backward and ignorant because they did not follow American customs. The pressure to conform gained momentum because the official policy of the school system coincided with that of native American school teachers.

Most second-generation Italian children used English to hide their teenage secrets from their parents. Many developed linguistic nonreciprocity, that is, they understood the Italian spoken by their parents but spoke only English. Author Mario Puzo wrote about the conflict he experienced in his New York City childhood when he discovered a new world in the New England countryside during summer Fresh Air Fund vacations. Wearing pajamas, eating American food, and observing the orderliness and quiet demeanor of the native American farm family he visited impressed him as superior to the way of life in his mother's tenement apartment. Puzo's afternoons spent at the library in the local settlement house took him away from his Italian immigrant surroundings into a world peopled by the characters of James Fenimore Cooper, Nathaniel Hawthorne, and Herman Melville. The people around him in New York's Hell's Kitchen seemed crude and backward. As a child he never saw Italians appreciating the beauty of the "American dream." He saw desperate men and women struggling on a mean level for existence. It was the example of another more valuable world that undermined the ways of second-generation Italian children and their respect for elders. The old ways seemed both quaint and inferior, and it was not until middle age, after his own success and security, that Puzo could view these lives differently.

For many Italian-American children the free public-school system served as the first step up the ladder of broader opportunity. In Puzo's experience it was "choosing a dream." He wanted to be a writer, but his mother opposed the idea because she believed it out of his reach. (In Italy only the nobility could aspire to such things.) But for the Puzo family life in America did in fact change, since Mrs. Puzo attained her goal of owning a home on Long Island, and her son became a very successful writer.

Other institutions such as the public health service, visiting nurses, hospital clinics, and charity workers brought into the Little Italies other aspects of American culture. Often the communication between the social service worker and the Italian immigrant was through a middle person—a relative or neighbor who was bilingual, or a school-age child serving as interpreter. Some agencies employed interpreters to assist in their work.

In such settlement houses as Addams' Hull House in Chicago, Europeans were encouraged to practice or exhibit their Old World crafts, literature, and music. Social reformers hoped to instill a respect for the Old World customs by singling them out for praise in an American setting, where they were appreciated for their beauty. In New York City an Italian lace-making school founded by socially prominent native women sought to combine the preservation of an Old World skill with profitable employment for immigrant women. (Although these skills were admired by the native American, they were seen as quaint vestiges of a time long past, and immigrant children preferred to see their parents move into modern times and act like modern Americans.)

Nevertheless, these native American institutions did provide a support system for the immigrants. They organized to provide services to improve the quality of life even if the context was American. In school the nurse taught children about personal hygiene and the teacher lectured on nutrition. Mothers learned modern methods of child care and home economics at the community centers. Women formed clubs where they combined sociability with sewing and other needlework, preserved cultural traditions, and more.

City, town, and county governments offered many employment opportunities—street repair, streetcar track maintenance, sanitation work, and sewer and drain construction and repair. Male laborers assigned to work for the city came into contact with native Americans and immigrants from other countries. In his home and on the street, the immigrant encountered politicians and party representatives who encouraged him to become a naturalized citizen and to take part in the elective system. The local committeeman also mediated between the immigrant community and the government bureaucracy. Securing a peddler's license, repairing the aftermath of a child's petty crime, obtaining municipal jobs, and smoothing over rent difficulties were some of the issues that fell into his realm of action. Thus, the American political process, organized on the precinct level, brought the immigrant into the public arena. Individual businessmen, lawyers, and employment agents discovered the benefits of political influence, which enabled them to obtain favors for their conationals. The ambitious, active men in the immigrant community joined the party ranks, recruited followers, and guided them on election day. In some towns and cities, Italian-American politicians earned elective office. Constantine Lauretta served as major of Mobile, Alabama, in 1846, and Vincent Palmisano won a seat on Baltimore's city council in 1915. Most of the political successes derived from a multiethnic coalition—a trade-off of support for candidates from different ethinic groups. Exposure to the American process of pressure politics intruded into the life of Little Italies and paved the way for a more involved interaction.

Problems of adjustment were not a simple matter of learning to dress, talk, and act like Americans. For the first generation, those Italian-born adults who emigrated to the United States, there was a wider contrast between the two cultures. Primary identity for most of them remained Italian. Even those who left their homeland because of *la miseria*, the frustrations of a life bound by legal traditions, did not repudiate their attachment to the familiar practices of family ties, interdependence through godparenthood, social deference established along lines of property owner-ship, skills, and education, and pride in the local history and folklore of their *paese.* Their dialects, food, values, and common experience sustained them along the barren stretches of railroad construction sites in South Da-kota, British Columbia, and in the bunkhouses of mining communities sprinkled among the farmlands of Oklahoma, Nebraska, Illinois, the small mill towns in Maine, and the fishing coasts of Pass Christian, Mississippi; Brownsville, Texas; Morgan City, Louisiana; and Monterey, California. For the majority of immigrants the institutions they developed in North America extended their ties to *Italianita* as they knew it. Immigrant insti-tutions, such as the Italian language press, the national parishes, the *paese* club, and the mutal benefit association, established new forms of identity. Those immigrants who decided to stay in America began to mix the two cultures. Even those who returned to Italy discovered that time spent abroad had altered attitudes and expectations about life.

Although the immigrant anticipated many hardships, he could not know the specific forms they would take. Throughout the nineteenth cen-tury and into the twentieth century, immigrants faced problems of nativ-ism, xenophobia, and discrimination. The floodtide of Italian immigration occurred at a time when the North American socioeconomic system was adjusting to the forces of industrialism and urbanization. Development and exploitation of the vast resources available required capital, technolog-ical expertise, a domestic market, and a cheap labor force. The waves of immigrants crossing the Atlantic or Pacific responded to the opportunities offered by industry and state, local, and national governments. These workers fitted into a system that viewed them as economic pieces—hands to dig the trenches, lay the railroad ties, and operate the mill equipment. Wages for labor were determined by the laws of supply and demand; em-ployers sought to keep all costs, especially labor, at a minimum and felt little responsibility toward the workers.

The Italians were only one of the many immigrant groups who suf-fered the disdain of the native population. In the 1850s native Americans had displayed signs in Boston reading, "Irish Need Not Apply." In 1856 the Know-Nothing party (also known as the American party) drafted a platform that proposed the end of immigration and made it difficult for foreigners to become naturalized citizens. In the 1870s groups of workers on the West Coast attacked Chinese laborers, whom they accused of dis-placing native Americans by accepting lower wages and unsafe working conditions.

Before the 1880s Italian immigrants did not attract specific condem-nation. Nativism or xenophobia occurred in North America during times of domestic crises and was usually aimed at a large, visible group of strang-ers who appeared to threaten time-honored traditions. The Catholicism of Irish and German immigrants and their custom of sociable drinking fright-ened both those natives who believed that Romanism would undermine Protestant values and those who believed that alcoholic consumption was evil and led to the corruption of society.

Before 1880 Italian colonies had grown gradually in such cities as New York, New Orleans, and San Francisco. These foreigners were pioneers who planned to settle permanently in America. Since many earned their living by providing goods and services to the English-speaking population, the emphasis for them was on acculturation—acquiring the language and customs of the host society, while perhaps maintaining some *Italianita*. The leaders of these communities supported the appreciation of Italian opera, art, and architecture. Like their American counterparts, they lived near their place of work and their occupations dispersed them throughout each community.

After 1880 the situation changed both for Italians and Americans. That year marks the turning point for immigration. Previously the bulk of immigrants originated in the northern and western nations of Europe (England, Scandinavia, the Low Countries, France, Germany); after 1880 individuals from the countries of southern and eastern Europe (the Balkans, the Baltic countries, the Russian and Austrian empires, Italy, Turkey) predominated. Post-1880 immigrants represented ethnocultures that differed dramatically from those who had come before.

Italians, Greeks, Jews, Poles, Serbs, and Finns concentrated in areas where there were available jobs. They crowded into mining, mill, and railroad towns and settled in the industrial/commercial sections of cities where they found work. The combination of numbers and concentration of settlement made the newcomers more visible and underscored their differentness. Most of these immigrants came to North America without resources and were forced to live cheaply and in substandard housing; they saved money to send back to Europe or to pay for the passage of relatives. Some came without skills and earned a meager wage in the street trades— peddler, bootblack, and street entertainer.

As the newcomers arrived, the American system appeared to be faltering. The expanding industrial capitalist system grew at an uneven pace. Cycles of prosperity, recession, and depression created anxiety for workers and management. The rapid growth of industrial centers placed a burden on housing, schools, law enforcement, and other institutions. A combination of factors, the most visible being the juxtaposition of dissimilar cultures, increased pressures and tensions caused by the social and economic uncertainties. While the immigrants did not create the economic situation they entered, their presence contributed to its growth for good and for bad. The same workers whose strong backs and willing hands enlarged the labor force also allowed the employers to manipulate them economically. The immigrants seemed eager to work for inadequate wages and to endure the discomforts of substandard housing and unsafe working conditions. Therefore, native Americans took advantage of the immigrants' desperation to cover financial obligations in their native country, their disposition to consider life in America as a temporary phenomenon, their dependence on the middleman *padrone* for jobs, and their interdependence on *paesani* for personal support and comfort.

Both native American capitalists and workers believed the immigrants responsible for the problems to which they contributed. They believed that the immigrants tolerated, as some variety of Mediterranean fatalism, the unsanitary housing and dangerous, low-paying jobs, endorsed the truancy and even delinquency of their children, endured the exploitation of conationals who overcharged *paesani* for food, stole their earnings through fraudulent banking, and engaged in extortion, kidnapping, and vendetta. They reasoned that the immigrants were accustomed to these low standards and perhaps even believed that these conditions in America were superior to those they left behind. The native Americans also suspected that all the attendant evils were part of the immigrants' baggage brought across the ocean. They accepted little responsibility for the domestic conditions that were in fact products of the system. Newspapers and magazines printed lurid accounts of the unsavory side of immigration. Most often their criticism exposed a double standard. They allowed immigrants the free choice of earning low wages, except when they feared this created unfair competition for native Americans. They ignored the problems of unsanitary and inadequate housing until the epidemics of the ethnic ghetto threatened the health of the native population. They resigned themselves to vendetta crime as long as the victims were immigrants. If, however, the victims were natives, the authorities rounded up anyone remotely suspected of the crime. The vigilante mentality of Americans hastened to punish those believed guilty. The sensational lynchings of Italians in the 1890s and the early decades of the twentieth century were condoned by the general public. A disregard for the human dignity of the immigrants occurred each day, as they were denied jobs and housing and ridiculed and slandered. A direct form of discrimination was the ethnic slurs—wop, dago, guinea, and mafiosi—while a more subtle form was the reinforcement of the stereotype of lower educational aspirations among immigrants, as school officials counseled children to take trade and commercial courses.

When the immigrants seemed disinterested in organizing against oppressive conditions, their native coworkers felt betrayed. Yet, when some of these immigrant workers attempted to use the class consciousness of European worker ideology, many natives believed them too militant. In fact, whenever foreigners were involved in violent labor disputes, they were charged with radicalism and un-Americanism. Natives ignored the domestic origins of these conditions, their own pioneer heritage of revolution against tyrannical conditions, and their own propensity to take justice into their own hands and to lash out against official and social oppression (such as the New York draft riots of 1863 and the Populist protest of the 1890s).

Italian immigrants were also criticized for focusing their concerns on events and conditions in Italy, such as their quickness to contribute to the relief of victims of natural disasters in Italy, their readiness to return to Italy to fight for *La Patria* in 1915, and their support for Italian national interests during the Versailles Conference of 1919. Italian immigrants were further criticized for sending money to their families in Italy rather than spending the money in America, for being slow to apply for citizenship, and for "selling" their votes to the local party boss.

But, by the 1920s, the nationality quotas of the immigration laws had drastically cut the flow from Italy, as well as other countries of southeastern Europe. Modest violations of Prohibition—such as making wine and selling it to *paesani* within the Little Italies—aroused almost the same indignation produced over the organized crime syndicates, which manufactured and sold alcohol on a large scale. Gangland wars, unfortunately, typified the entire community. Bugs Moran and Dutch Schultz notwithstanding, somehow crime became an Italian thing. The arrest in 1920 of Nicola Sacco and Bartolomeo Vanzetti for a payroll holdup and murder, their conviction the following year, and their execution in 1927 highlighted this negative combination.

While many well-known American writers, educators, and politicians admired and praised the emergence to power of Benito Mussolini in the 1920s, most began to question his imperial goals for Italy and his friendliness with Adolf Hitler in the 1930s. Many Italian Americans basked in the glory and success of Mussolini because he had made Italy into a respected world power, and Italy's sons and daughters abroad felt proud to be an indirect part of that achievement.

The infatuation of some Italian Americans with fascism in turn contributed to conflict and violence in America. Within the Italian-American community were those opposed to the regime in Italy and its propaganda efforts. The opposition drew its strength from the small pockets of political radicals who fought against all forms of fascism. These few were joined by individuals who questioned the loss of liberty in the Italian state and opposed Mussolini's expansionist policies. Dissension ranged from arguments and debates to written diatribes, public meetings, and rallies. Heated words sometimes led to open fighting. Americans disdained both extremes as suspect. But, as the Axis powers formed an alliance that threatened world peace, Americans suspected Italian Americans of split loyalties. Anti-Italian sentiment strengthened with the outbreak of war in Europe and Italy's invasion of France in 1940. President Roosevelt's description of this action as a dagger in the back angered many of the Italian Americans who then voted for the Republican candidate for president, Wendell L. Willkie, in 1940.

On the eve of World War II, many Americans questioned the loyalty of Italian Americans to the United States. Once Italy declared war against America, Italian immigrants became enemy aliens. Midnight raids led by the FBI rounded up those who had spoken or written in favor of fascism, those who had shortwave radios, and those who resided in military security areas (along the coasts).

Most Italian Americans did not falter in their immediate commitment to the American cause. Sons of immigrants enlisted or reported to draft boards with the blessings of their parents. The fine line between hostility and acceptance was crossed as Italian-American organizations held bond drives and did their part to help win the war for America.

During the 1930s and 1940s children of immigrants faced the subtle discrimination of socioeconomic origin. Firms that did not hire Jews often also felt uncomfortable hiring Catholics whose names ended in vowels. Promotion on the basis of merit somehow seemed tied to having an American surname. The second generation straddled the barrier to acceptance. The choice seemed for some to be as simple as changing their name, moving away from the old neighborhood, or marrying a non-Italian. Certainly, their interaction with American institutions, organizations, government, politics, the armed forces, the church, and unions expanded their new self-concept.

All non–Anglo-Saxon American groups have experienced some measure of suspicion and prejudice. Each group has sought ways of coping with it. Italian Americans developed a varied approach. In San Francisco, Sicilian fishermen protested against an increase in their license tax; in 1912 Italian Americans helped elect Fiorello La Guardia to represent New York in the U.S. Congress; and in Lawrence, Massachusetts, in 1912 Italians initiated and were prominent organizers in the strike against the injustices of the mill operators.

Battered and bruised, misused and exploited, the majority of the immigrants faced each moment with hardened determination. They endured without abandoning all the amenities of life. They created support with the *paese* boardinghouse over a game of cards; they re-created the extended family that welcomed friends as well as relatives; they found companionship at work and at the street markets where the world became a town piazza; they sought out *paesani* and fellow Italians to join sports clubs, dramatic groups, social and religious associations.

On the job they began to develop tactics of cooperation. Many joined craft unions and helped to form the industrial unions; many also led the efforts for union organization. Italian-American entrepreneurs also sought to ease the burden of risky working conditions. Barbers, shoemakers, and other artisans formed social groups that offered some health benefits; Italian fruit merchants, fishermen, and strawberry growers formed cooperatives to share the risk of uncertain markets and natural disasters.

Instead of perpetuating a separateness from the American mainstream, the efforts to order and direct their lives brought them further into American society. Parallel forms of life strategies developed for each ethnic group. Italians found themselves a social mirror as the American technique of linking interest groups brought them into contact with all peoples. The Italian celebration of Columbus Day, which served to remind Americans of the Genovese who discovered the New World, was preempted by the Americans who credited Columbus with launching the European nations on their efforts to colonize and civilize the wilderness.

The second and especially the third generation continued to infiltrate the American mainstream. They shared their birthright, their education, their future with all Americans. What remained as Italian was a modification, a dilution of the culture taken from the *paese* in the 1870s. By the 1950s an increase in intermarriage, an increase in educational achievement and income, and the movement of Italians to the suburbs seemed to signal the end of ethnicity. What remained was nostalgia, a caricature of things remembered. What lay ahead appeared to be amalgamation, homogenization, the culmination of the melting pot.

Italian Americans had made it. In politics, business, the arts, education, they had come into their own. A cavalcade of well-known individuals whose identity was acknowledged by all Americans meant acceptance of the larger group. Such open recognition of Americans with ethnic names emerged at a time when the country was more aware of past guilt in the treatment of minorities. During the 1960s the Civil Rights Act reaffirmed America's commitment to equality, and affirmative action legislation enabled many individuals to aspire to the top positions. In 1965 Congress amended the discriminatory immigration legislation of the 1920s that had established nationality quotas. Italians, along with other southeastern European groups, were low on that list, which gave priority to peoples from the northwestern European countries. Within the United States, the civil rights movement and the demand for black studies and bilingualism for Hispanics set up a response among other ethnics. Cultural pluralism rather than the melting pot now dominated the philosophy of the politicians and the educators. Millions of Americans began to seek their roots and found that their shared cultural traditions did not devalue their American identity.

In Canada in 1950 a major influx of postwar immigrants renewed Old World ties. The newcomers were products of a modern Italian society familiar with pressure politics and determined to maintain their Italian heritage. In Canadian cities of Italian settlement, bilingualism was legislated.

The civil rights movement also gave impetus to ethnic self-awareness. Every ethnic group in American history had protested against its mistreatment, but the pattern of the 1950s and 1960s encouraged a more formal, organized national campaign. Ethnic organizations employed the media, organized rallies, picketed government offices, and bombarded politicians with petitions. Some began to ask for a greater share in the American dream. Surveys were made of the "executive suite" to see if all Americans enjoyed their "fair" (potential) piece of the sources of power. Antidefamation became a conscious part of each group's policy. Asians picketed against the Charlie Chan image; Hispanics protested against the Frito Bandito; Poles resented the Polish Joke Book. At the same time each group accelerated its cultural and educational activities. Ethnic historical societies blossomed, ethnic journals flourished, and scholars in all disciplines from language to history to anthropology turned full attention toward the immigrant/ethnic experience in America. For the Italians these associations included the American Italian Historical Association, the Italian American Anti Defamation League, the National Italian American Foundation, and the journal *Italian Americana.*

This outbreak of activity among the ranks of the ethnic leaders filtered down to the general public. As scholars researched the lives of the immigrants, they began to collect documents, letters, photos, and printed materials. Many immigrants were interviewed and asked to describe the events of the past, ones they had either experienced or learned about from others. The process of collecting, gathering, interpreting, and publicizing often expanded into a community effort as members of families became amateur historians. To the surprise of many people they discovered that instead of considering themselves assimilated the majority of Italian Americans maintained a connection with their cultural heritage. They began to demonstrate their curiosity by subscribing to the popular magazines *IAM* and *Identity.* They attended historical conferences. They began to ask for books on Italian subjects at their libraries. While Italian Americans felt this sense of continuity, it was mostly emotional and psychological; often a third- or fourth-generation person could not explain why he or she felt part of both cultures.

Marcus Lee Hansen, a famous historian of ethnicity, once suggested that the third generation would record the experience of their grandparents. He believed that the awkward self-consciousness that haunted many of the second generation made objective self-examination painful and difficult, if not impossible. He thought that the third generation's confidence in belonging to America would allow them to venture bravely into their past. They would question their parents about the family's history. Most often the parents could not answer these questions because they had been too busy making their way into American society or had felt the need to forget the old in order to adopt the new. The third generation's frustration would serve as a stimulus for them to visit greataunts, check through family trunks, take courses in family history, or decide to pursue graduate training in the humanities and social sciences to learn the tools of professional research. And many of the studies now in the libraries come from the pens of these descendants of immigrants.

The desire of people to know about their past in an effort to understand their present lives better is as old as human society. The true coming of age of any group is the moment when it can look at its past, the glories and successes, as well as the warts and blemishes, with an open mind. For the Italian American this has meant the maturity to appreciate the contributions of the "little people," the inarticulate laborers who dug the New York City subways or who toiled in the canneries of California and Massachusetts. This has meant the ability to accept the wide range of Italian influence in American life—from the anarchists and the labor organizers to the pro-fascists and the bootleggers. With the bittersweetness of maturity comes the gratification over the hard-earned achievement of having built huge family businesses from storefronts or pushcarts, and the pride that results from the success of contemporary Italian Americans who bring their sensitivity to ethnic identity into their politics, their literature, their cinematography, their art. The process of self-appreciation remains alive and positive as it builds on the present and plans for the future. Italian Americans today are charting their recent and personal past and present in much the same way that Cabot, Verrazzano, Malispina, and Columbus charted the sea lanes and coasts of North America. The joy of self-discovery and self-celebration has brought a new dimension to the lives of Italian Americans that reflects the uniqueness of American society.

San Francisco, 1982

SETTLEMENT 1

1. Il centro (downtown) Introdaqua, Abruzzi, in 1900. The pattern of
agricultural settlement differed in the Old World. Rather than living on their
own homesteads, as in America, farmers and peasants lived in the villages,
where houses were close to each other, and walked to the fields each day. *Paese*
life included a rich variety of occupations and reflected an urban class structure.

Migration was a way of life for Italians throughout the nineteenth century. They traveled within the Italian peninsula, to other areas of Europe, and to North Africa in search of work. Laboring in the mines and factories of industrial areas, they provided the artisan skills needed to construct and embellish the expanding cities.

Since the political, social, and economic divisions within the Italian peninsula prevented cooperative development, each area had its own problems and separate history, customs, and dialect. Even so, Italian nationalists fought and schemed to unite the nation. Efforts for unification precipitated political action culminating in demonstrations and revolutions. The civil authorities, as we see in Puccini's opera *Tosca*, relentlessly pursued organizers as common criminals. Italy's political refugees sought safety in Europe. Some fled as far as the New World.

Emigration from Italy increased in proportion to internal conditions and external opportunities. In the 1860s and 1870s, thousands of *conta-*

dini (farmers) left the regions of Lombardy, Venezia, and Emilia. They emigrated to South America, especially Brazil and Argentina. Changes in agricultural tenure and cultivation plus industrialization acted as a stimulus to their departure. The desire of Brazil and Argentina to develop their natural resources prompted their adoption of an immigration policy that offered free passage to prospective settlers.

In the 1880s and 1890s, conditions in southern Italy deteriorated as natural disasters, such as phylloxera (a disease attacking grape vines), spread, and the population suffered from the trade wars with European nations that cut off foreign markets for agricultural produce. Increases in taxation also weighed heavily on a region in which exchange was often in kind or services rather than cash and earnings were low. Emigrants from the south headed for North America, where rapid industrialization created opportunities for employment.

Improvements in technology also affected transatlantic travel. Steamship companies reduced their rates as a result of increased competition, efficiency, and speed of travel. Advertisements emphasized the low rates and ease of travel. Many Italian men were able to go abroad to work each year and return to Italy with their earnings. Many early American colonies were formed when Italian seamen, usually Genovese, settled in the ports they visited while transporting cargo for European and American clients.

Preparations for departure included obtaining a passport and a certificate listing a male's military status. Emigrants traveled to the nearest port of departure, and trade routes from these ports channeled traffic to New World destinations. Although transatlantic transportation was relatively inexpensive (approximately $30), travel accommodations in steerage were far from adequate. Below deck 300 to 600 people occupied open sleeping quarters. Each bunk averaged 30 cubic feet of space, and primitive sanitary conditions, seasickness, and overcrowding transformed steerage into a horrid place. Weather permitting, passengers spent most of their time above deck.

Arrival in America held many fears for new Americans. Most immigrants from Italy arrived in New York and entered through Ellis Island, the immigration station opened in 1891. There the men were separated from the women and children, but all were subjected to medical examinations and interrogation. Between 1897 and 1913, thousands of Italians arrived at Ellis Island. If they passed examinations and gained admission, they were ferried to the Battery section of New York City or to New Jersey train terminals to continue their journey to places across the continent.

Enterprising Italian Americans offered services to their arriving co-nationals. They could exchange money, provide transportation, recommend boardinghouses and hotels, or offer employment. Some of these individuals were unscrupulous and cheated the unwary. Authorities attempted to circumvent this problem by providing some of these services at Ellis Island or by referring immigrants to charitable agencies. Organized by the local Italian-American community and subsidized by the Italian government, these agencies dealt with the personal difficulties of each newcomer.

Both chance and strategy determined the final destination of Italian immigrants. Men seeking work traveled to areas where opportunities beckoned. Immigrants mined iron and copper in the upper Midwest; constructed and maintained railroads in every region in North America; fished the gulf coasts of Texas and Louisiana, the coasts of Monterey and San Francisco, and along the Atlantic coast; and farmed in Oregon, California, Illinois, New Jersey, and Louisiana. Some of these skills were learned in Italy, while others were acquired in America. Once a small nucleus of Italians settled in a community, others followed. Letters written to family and friends back home described this "America" of Pittston, Pennsylvania; Donaldsonville, Louisiana; Hibbing, Minnesota; and North Bay, Ontario, to prospective emigrants. As these communities increased in size, they in turn created business opportunities for Italian Americans who specialized in such ethnic enterprises as importing and retailing Italian products.

From the days of the explorers until well into the twentieth century, the Italian presence touched every region of Canada and the United States. Concentrations of immigrants grew where jobs and Italian Americans intersected and established an *ambiente*. The Little Italies of American cities recreated the *paese* or town atmosphere of the Old World. But even in far-off places like Helper, Utah, and White Cloud, Kansas, Italians sought the company of other Italians or native Americans to share the food, wine, and celebration of life that were important to the immigrant.

2. Italian street scene. Towns served as the economic centers of a region. Agricultural produce and manufactured products were offered for sale, but many people bartered for goods rather than purchased them.

3. Contadini posing with their agricultural implements. Although Italian *contadini* (peasant farmers) were accustomed to intensive agricultural methods, economic conditions worked against the adoption of modern agricultural techniques. Landowners preferred to accrue their annual profit rather than invest in long-term production.

4. Women working in the fields of Calabria. Life for the *contadini* required the involvement of the entire family. Children worked at an early age, and women, local customs permitting, labored in the fields, especially during harvesting.

5. Sicilian fishermen catching tuna.
The Mediterranean provided food and
work for Italians along Italy's extensive
coast. America's fishing and wholesale-
retail fish industry attracted immigrants
with such backgrounds.

6. Pasta vendors of Naples.

7. Calabrese farm workers, about 1925. Modernization of Italian agriculture developed in the twentieth century, spurred on by the spread of industrialization, the need to produce more food for a growing urban population and foreign markets, and to compensate for the loss of farm workers who emigrated.

8. A cigarette factory in Florence. Italian industry developed in the late nineteenth century in the northern sections of the nation, particularly in Piedmont, Lombardy, and Emilia—especially the processing of raw materials that were usually imported. For example, in 1891 this factory manufactured cigarettes from tobacco grown in the American South.

9. A municipal bakery in Catania, Sicily, in 1904. Bakers of bread and *dolci* (pastries) emigrated to America and established businesses serving Italian-American communities and later attracted the patronage of other ethnic groups. Many other Italian immigrants were artisans, shoemakers, cabinetmakers, barbers, and weavers.

10. Canning factory in Nocera Inferiore (near Naples). This factory produced products for domestic consumption as well as for export. Italian Americans imported tomatoes, olive oil, cheeses, and fish from Italy. Some made contracts with companies that imported food under their own labels, such as Sole D'Italia, which was registered by a Philadelphia company before World War I. In the 1940s the name was transferred to a distributor in Baltimore, Maryland.

11. Strikers at the labor headquarters at Torre Annunziata, Naples. Italy's industrial workers faced the problems of an economic system that viewed labor as a cost factor. Poor working conditions and low wages increased tensions, which broke out in demonstrations of unrest. Socialist theories that supported the concept of social and economic justice for all people appealed to many who fought against a system that seemed to exploit the workers. Some immigrants brought this heightened political consciousness with them to America, where they became active in labor organizing and in alternative political movements, ranging from anarchism to communism.

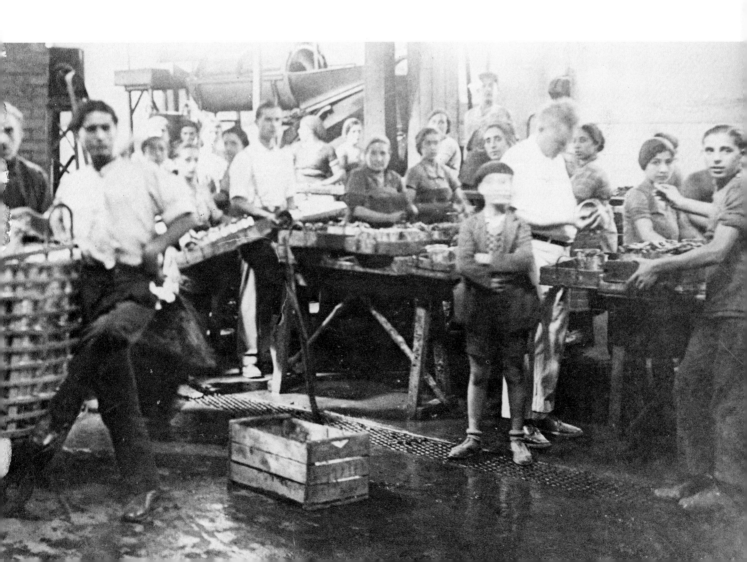

12. Carabinieri subdue a rebellious group in Naples in 1893. Strikes and demonstrations did not always occur among industrial workers. In the early 1890s peasants in central Sicily protested against landholding policies and taxes. They stormed municipal buildings and burned records. As the price of bread increased, peasants in the south raided bakeries and pillaged local shops and grain elevators. The riots spread northward. In industrial cities like Milan, workers joined the demonstrations. The government retaliated by sending out troops to suppress the reactionaries. In such confrontations throughout Italy, many people were arrested and some were killed.

13. Street urchins in Naples. Population increased in Italy in the late nineteenth and early twentieth centuries. For many this meant that meager agricultural resources were insufficient. In addition, trade wars between European nations, the competition from the developing citrus industry in the United States, and the devastation from disease of the grape harvests placed further burdens upon an already troubled nation. Idleness was an alternative to emigration. Street urchins lived by their nimble fingers and quick wits.

14. Palm Sunday procession in Benevento, about 1925. Elaborate expressions of religious belief combined devotion with communal life, and *paesani* united to prepare for these annual celebrations. Emigrants carried with them to the New World the ties they had formed in Italy.

15. Funeral procession in Roseto degli Abruzzi in the 1920s. Attendance at funerals reflected the respect, loyalty, and obligation of one's neighbors, friends, and relatives. One's life belonged to the family and then to the community.

16. Departure for America. Not all emigrants left Italy because of poverty or disappointment with conditions. Some left to face the challenge of a new experience. Frank Mei and Amadeo Enrico Santini posed for this picture in 1913 in their hometown of Avezzano, Aquila, Italy. Both were eighteen and wanted to come to the United States to seek their fortunes. Their parents opposed their decision but finally surrendered to their sons' desire for adventure.

15

17. Partenza degli emigranti. This painting by A. Tommasi depicts emigrants awaiting departure. Until 1870 most Italians emigrated to South America rather than North America—especially to the countries of Brazil and Argentina. As of 1860 only 14,000 Italians had migrated to the United States. The flood of emigration to the United States began in 1880; this is the period from which most Americans of Italian heritage originate.

19. Military service certificate. This certificate indicates that Angelo Valerioti from Cosenza had completed his military duty and was thus eligible to emigrate to America.

18. The port of Genoa in the late nineteenth century served as one point of embarkation for emigrants. Genovese seamen were among the first Italians to cross the ocean and settle in America's cities. They transported cargo for clients in Wales, Germany, Australia, and America. Many major port cities in America housed these Italian sailors between voyages. Some remained as ship chandlers and importers and developed a commercial link between Europe and America.

20. Immigration detention quarters in Trieste. American immigration laws required that individuals who were ineligible for admission because of their health, financial status, or undesirable condition (such as a criminal) be transported back to Europe at the expense of the steamship companies that brought them to America. In order to reduce their liability, ports of debarkation established facilities for examining immigrants before they left Europe. This immigration detention quarters maintained by Cosulich in Trieste had 1,080 beds.

18

21. Ticket to America. Maria Cristofoli from Casarsa, Udine, purchased a third-class ticket for passage on the *Duca degli Abruzzi*, scheduled to sail from Genoa to New York (via Naples) in October 1919.

22. Steerage deck of the S.S. *Pennland*, circa 1893. The majority of the four million Italians who journeyed to America between 1865 and 1914 traveled in steerage class, where passengers slept and lived in rows of double-decker bunks, 6 feet long, 2 feet wide, and 2$\frac{1}{2}$ feet apart. The trip from Naples to New York, Boston, or Philadelphia usually took two to three weeks. The closeness and discomfort of steerage drove passengers to the outside deck.

23. Advertising America. Steamship companies and their ticket agents advertised their services to Italians already in America. Chiariglione and Massari of Pueblo, Colorado, placed this advertisement in their local newspaper in 1923. They claimed forty years of experience in arranging transportation for those wishing to return to Italy or those who wished to bring their relatives and friends to America.

24. Island of Tears. Ellis Island was called *Isola delle Lagrime* (Island of Tears) by many Italians. Each immigrant was subject to medical examination and interrogation to determine if he or she had violated the strict immigration laws. All new arrivals feared this stage of their journey. They knew that families could be separated and individuals detained for further examination or deported.

25. Ferry to Ellis Island. Immigrants were transported from their ships by ferry to Ellis Island, located in Upper New York Bay. This Italian family rides the ferry in 1905 to Ellis Island, where they would be examined for admission to America.

26. Immigrants from the *Princess Irene* line up at Ellis Island in 1911. Some of these men had been to America before. Throughout the nineteenth century Italian laborers had traveled each season to work in the countries of Europe and North Africa. As North American industry developed, they expanded their itinerary.

27. Waiting for processing at Ellis Island. Once men were separated from women, all immigrants waited for hours to file through the various processing lines. They were examined for contagious diseases and lice. Their passports were examined and they were questioned about the amount of money they had, potential employment, and their destinations.

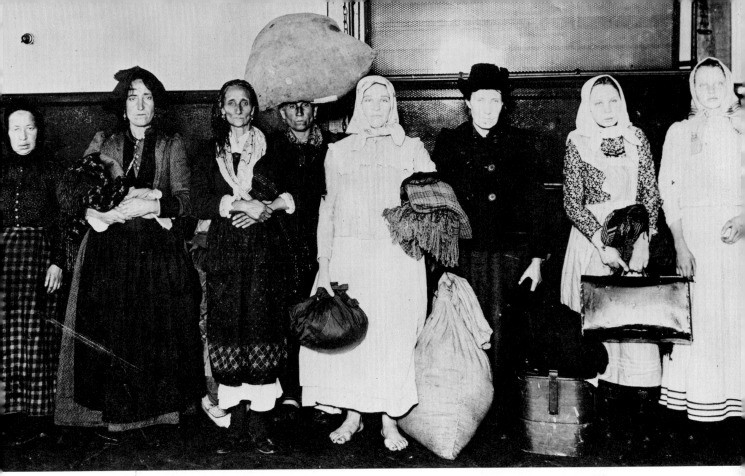

28. Female immigrants. Women unaccustomed to public examinations felt frightened and humiliated as they were ordered to undress and stand in line for medical examinations.

29. Return to Italy. According to U.S. law, those immigrants likely to become public charges were ineligible for admission to America. Here indigent Italians are returned to Genoa, where they are met by repatriation officials.

23

30. Railroad waiting room. These Italians wait for the railroad ferry at Ellis Island that will take them to rail terminals in Hoboken and Jersey City. From those terminals they would journey to points beyond New York.

31. Immigrants in New York City. Once the processing was complete, immigrants settling in New York City were ferried across the harbor to the barge office at the Battery. Once they passed these gates, they were on their own.

32. Battery Park. Men crowded around the disembarkation areas at Battery Park offering to help carry luggage, advertising hotels, and offering transportation. Sometimes they spoke the same dialect as the incoming Italian and convinced him that they were trustworthy countrymen or *paesani*. Many immigrants were prey to the unscrupulous practices of these "runners." Even the most straightforward and impersonal offer of services followed the rules of supply and demand. The driver in this picture demands payment before taking this arriving immigrant woman to her destination.

25

33. Hotels catered to individual ethnic groups and specific regions of the homeland. Antonio Solari, the proprietor of the Hotel Ticino in New York City, encouraged the patronage of Italian Swiss. He also advertised in an 1881 almanac of Italian-Swiss Americans published in San Francisco so that he could attract the trade of returning immigrants or their relatives traveling to join them.

34. The Liberty Hotel. P. Raho, proprietor of the Liberty Hotel in New York City, claimed that his establishment was recommended by steamship agents.

35. Railroad companies advertised in periodicals purchased by the immigrants. This advertisement lists the cities served by the railroad that had Italian communities along its route and shows connections both west and east of Chicago.

36. Mulberry Street. Italians settled all across America. After 1890 the heaviest concentrations were in the cities of the Northeast. In 1930 New York City had 1,070,355 persons of Italian birth or parentage. Jacob Riis photographed this outdoor market on Mulberry Street in 1906 in New York's Little Italy. The closeness of houses and street commerce somewhat resembled the housing pattern and outdoor living of Italian cities.

27

37. The Hotel Rome, located at North Square in Boston's Little Italy, at the turn of the century. These same streets had echoed the ride of Paul Revere. Boston, like many American cities, housed its immigrants in its oldest, run-down sections.

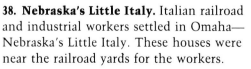

38. Nebraska's Little Italy. Italian railroad and industrial workers settled in Omaha—Nebraska's Little Italy. These houses were near the railroad yards for the workers.

39. Pittsburgh's Italians. Italian immigrants arrived in America as the economy moved into an industrial expansion. Work was available in the factories, mills, mines, railroads, and canals. The Italians of Pittsburgh, like Italians elsewhere, established familiar settings in their new environment.

40. Minnesota Italians. An Italian-American home in St. Paul, Minnesota, in 1925. Some immigrants settled near the levees they helped maintain along the Mississippi River; others worked on the railroad that provided transportation to and from this major food-processing city.

41. Carlos Gentile, an Italian photographer who traveled throughout the American West, adopted an orphaned Yauapai Apache boy in Arizona around 1870. He named his son Carlos Montezuma and took him to Chicago, where the boy studied medicine. Carlos became a doctor and a well-known advocate of Indian rights.

42. Italian settlers in San Francisco originally responded to the gold rush lure of 1849. By the turn of the century, Columbus Avenue was the main thoroughfare of Italian settlement in North Beach. This photo shows merchants along the avenue assessing the damage to their businesses immediately following the 1906 earthquake.

43. Texas Italians. Italians worked as fishermen, dockhands, and farmers in Galveston, Texas. These shrimpboats are moored at Grasso's pier.

44. Felix Pedro, born Felice Pedroni in Trignano di Fanano, Italy, arrived in America about 1881. He worked as a section hand on railroads in Illinois, Colorado, Utah, and Oregon. He mined coal at Carbonado, Washington, and then tried his luck at gold prospecting in Canada's Cariboo mountains. He traveled to the Yukon in 1894, often hiking alone, and probably was one of the first "white men" to prospect in what is now Fairbanks, Alaska. He discovered gold in 1902, and the news of his success resulted in the founding of that major Alaskan city.

45. The Italian North Bay Premier Band members settled in Ontario to work on railroad and canal construction and maintenance; others found employment in the mining camps.

46. Joe and John Fassino from Canischio, Italy, came to the section of Indian Territory that is now Oklahoma in the 1890s to supply Italian groceries to their fellow Italians, who were mainly miners. By 1897 they expanded their business interest by opening a macaroni factory in McAlester. Their market included Oklahoma, Kansas, Texas, Missouri, and Arkansas, with surplus sales sent to the Caribbean.

35

47. La Madonna Del Carmine, a wooden church in Asti, California, was built in the middle of the vineyards by the Italian wine makers.

48. Italian produce. Many Italian farmers brought their knowledge of produce to the commercial opportunities of street peddling—a trade that attracted immigrants who had raised many of these crops in Italy and one that required a small capital investment. In time, many peddlers advanced from pushcarts or horse and buggy to open trucks. This peddler drove his truck through the streets of Cleveland, Ohio, in the 1920s.

49. A squatters' neighborhood called "Mexico" in Pueblo, Colorado, first
housed families from New Mexico who worked in the smelting companies. In
the late nineteenth century Italian families began to settle there because they
were attracted to Colorado's mining industry. This family of "Mexico" lived in
the vicinity of a smelter, an establishment for separating metal.

50. Migrant workers. Italians were also migrant workers who left the city during the summer to harvest crops in the rural areas of New York, New England, New Jersey, Delaware, and Louisiana. Ann Parion, thirteen, and Andenito Carro, fourteen, picked berries at Newton's Farm in Cannon, Delaware around 1910. They traveled from Philadelphia each summer with their mothers to live and work in the fields. In Italy women carried baskets of fruit or wheat and jars of water on their heads. (Boxes of berries ranged in weight from 25 to 60 pounds.)

2

SOCIAL, CULTURAL, AND FAMILY LIFE

51. Marriage Italian style. Bernardina Falvo and Thomas Bonacci were married in Helper, Utah, in 1917. The choice of marriage partners was dictated by family and friends as well as geographical circumstances. One man described how he met his wife when he traveled to St. Louis to visit his uncle. The family of his wife-to-be lived upstairs, and although they had never met, they both came from the same town in Italy. This *paesani* connection plus a romantic attraction brought the pair to the altar.

Often the transition from sojourner to permanent resident in America depended upon the establishment of family life. The majority of migrants were men without women, alone in a strange land seeking work to earn money needed for families still in Italy. The decision to reunite the family by sending for mothers, sisters, wives, and fiancées, and the decision to start a family by having relatives in Italy choose a bride to send to America or by returning to Italy to choose a wife, were the basic motivations for developing a fuller life in America.

Italian-American communities reflected much of the regional culture that the immigrants brought with them, but their exposure to America also influenced the ways in which they responded to the conditions of daily life. Any attempt to recreate the Old World existence met the challenge of New World circumstances: What emerged was a structure tempered by selective accommodation.

In many ethnic groups, the family is the group through which the

41

past is preserved and the values and customs that govern society are continued. The Italian family in America remained a source of this conservation, but individual members also came into contact with the larger American society. Men found jobs that exposed them to non-Italians; their language expanded by incorporating English words, such as job (*jobba*) and boss (*bossa*). Even the women, who stayed home and seldom ventured beyond the geographic boundaries of *paesani* stores and the neighborhood, had to deal with non-Italians. No neighborhood remained the exclusive territory of any one group. The Little Italies of North America also housed Irish, Jewish, and Polish Americans, and most immigrant women communicated, in however limited fashion, with their next-door neighbors, their landlords, and the non-Italian dry goods store proprietor. Both mother and father had to adjust to children who spoke to each other in English at home—sometimes in defiance of parents who could not understand them. Parents faced a school system that encouraged children to regard non-American tradition as obsolete and a society that simultaneously respected Italian opera but often discriminated against the immigrant artisan barber, shoemaker, or baker who hummed arias from *Rigoletto*.

Within the context of family and community, Italian immigrants developed a social and cultural life that provided opportunities to enjoy the comfort of familiar sights, sounds, and smells, and to foster the cultural expression of the people. Most immigrants entertained relatives and close friends at home. Women would sit outside their houses and chat, while children played in the crowded streets. Men would stop at a friend's home or a saloon and spend a few hours playing cards and drinking wine. The growing, preparation, and sharing of food dominated the lives of most Italians, who made each meal a social event.

Organ grinders, hurdy-gurdy players, and local musicians filled the streets with music. As a livelihood, street entertainment was common in southern Italian cities. Puppet shows in the tradition of La Commedia Dell' Arte delighted the viewer. Italian musicians, among the earliest immigrants to America, played in the municipal and armed forces' bands and taught their skills to others. Musicians also formed bands to play at christenings, weddings, and public celebrations. Most families had at least one member who played the mandolin, the accordion, or the violin.

Local amateur groups scheduled performances of Italian opera and plays, and professional entertainers also catered to the immigrant community. Comedians, notably Farfariello, characterized familiar American types, such as the city policeman.

Although the immigrant community generated many of its own institutions and organizations, America's schools and reform groups attempted to direct the newcomers toward assimilation. Schools taught children and adults the symbols of America. George Washington and Thomas Jefferson replaced Giuseppe Garibaldi and Giuseppe Mazzini as folk heroes. American values and tastes appeared to second-generation children as modern and superior. In some cases the school experience interpreted immigrant culture as quaint, backward, and ignorant. Native American teachers often could not appreciate a way of life that they did not understand, and they believed their "mission" was to convince their students to accept the goals of the larger society.

The settlement house also entered into the immigrant community, offering various services to its residents. Settlement workers, although dedicated, believed that the old ways, while quaint, must make way for the new. Mothers learned how to bottle-feed babies and were scolded for applying whiskey to the gums of teething infants. Settlement houses provided a number of basic needs, such as milk for babies and child-care centers. They were places for teenagers to gather, for children to read books, and for men to learn English. They, too, sought to help ease the transition from alien to citizen.

Despite the contrasts between old and new, Italians chose the American customs they found useful and ignored the suggestions that threatened to undermine their basic values of family and tradition. Out of this interaction grew the culture of the Italian Americans.

52. Marriage Italian-American style. This elaborate wedding banquet in Detroit's Book Cadillac Hotel in 1925 attempted to merge the Old World with the New. Anthony Battaglia and Catherine Cianciolo decided to use tropical plants and flowers to give a Sicilian *ambiente* to the ornate ballroom, which was already enhanced with marble arches and balconies and white wrought-iron railings.

53. The author's parents. Antonina Gerardi and Francesco Scarpaci celebrated their wedding on April 15, 1928. They met on a blind date, but their courtship was allowed to continue under family supervision. Both fathers shared the cost of the reception, and Francesco's cousin designed and made the wedding gown.

54. A LaFata wedding. Giovanni LaFata and his wife, Concetta Mercurio, posed in the second row, extreme left and right, at their 1904 wedding. The parents, sisters, and brothers of Giovanni (who changed his name to John) complete the group. Young Salvatore LaFata holds a photo of his oldest sister, Pietrina, who could not attend the wedding.

55. A LaFata anniversary. In 1929 John and Concetta attended the golden anniversary celebration of John's parents, Giovanni LaFata and Agatha Randazzo LaFata, who were married in Terrasini, Sicily, on April 7, 1879. The *Detroit Free Press* reported the celebration, which included the LaFatas' four sons, four daughters, fifty-four grandchildren, and fourteen great-grandchildren.

56. The Cellas' American home. The majority of Italian immigrants came from *contadini* backgrounds. They were poor and in America dedicated their lives to *pane e lavoro* (bread and work). Families lived in crowded, often dilapidated housing in the older sections of the cities. Three rooms often housed eleven people, and the kitchen, with its coal stove, served as the central area for most activities. The family of Desiderio Cella, at 11 Coburn Street in South Framingham, Massachusetts, used the kitchen table to tie tags and to dry macaroni.

47

57. The Paresses' American home. The Paresse family gather in their kitchen at 4 Fly Street, Buffalo, New York. During the summer, Mrs. Paresse and her children worked in the Albion Canning Factory sheds on beans, peas, and corn. Six-year-old Joe was too small to get the husks off the corn, so his contributions to the family income were limited.

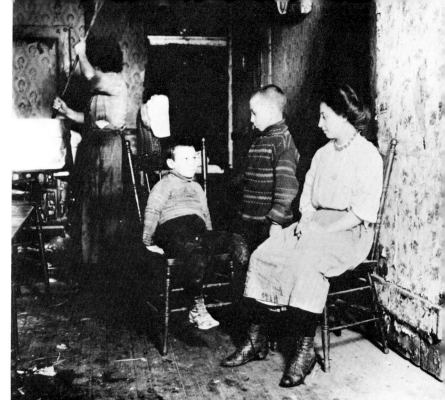

58. An Italian-American belle. Anita Palladino of Albuquerque, New Mexico, posed for this picture in 1900. Her father was a builder who came from the Abruzzi first to Maryland and then to Santa Fe, New Mexico, in the late 1860s. She married Tuscan-born Elia Gradi, and in 1913 they moved back to Gradi's hometown, Vicopelago, Lucca. Some of their children later emigrated to America.

59. Hartford, Connecticut. These newly arrived immigrants came to Hartford in March 1909 from Messina, Sicily, which had been devastated by an earthquake the previous December. Many of these men would find work constructing Hartford's streetcar tracks.

60. An Italian house in Detroit. The Mercurio and LaFata families had this house built in 1916 next to their grocery store on East Lafayette Street in Detroit. The balcony, corniced door, and tile roof represented Italianate architectural features.

61. An Italian-American kitchen. This replica of a typical 1920s Italian-American kitchen was part of the Nation of Nations Exhibit at the Smithsonian Institution. Most of the items, collected from families, were made in America, but some, like the pizzelle iron on the stove, have Italian origins. In this kitchen, New World utensils fashioned Italian meals made with ingredients usually imported from Italy. For the immigrants and their children, the kitchen served as the central focus for the family and its ritual gatherings for the sharing of food, wine, and talk.

62. The Italian-American wife. The Italian wife did her household chores for the welfare of her family. Every task, from hanging out the whitest sheets in the neighborhood to serving home-prepared pasta, reflected upon her family and then upon herself. Here Mrs. D'Annunzio irons in her upstate New York farmhouse.

63. Family gathering. Family, *paesani,* and close friends gathered together on Sundays and holidays. This 1930 scene from Baltimore, Maryland, shows the Matricianni and De Antoniis families from the Abruzzi. Mrs. Matricianni had cared for *paesani* boarders in order to save money to purchase this home in Little Italy.

64. First-generation Americans in Omaha. Omaha, Nebraska, was a midwestern community that attracted Italians to work on the railroads. Here an Italian couple rest after a hard day's work in 1940. Families tended vegetable gardens around the modest housing that was typical of the Italian section of the city.

65. Hauling supplies in Nevada. Joe B. Ferretta's team hauled supplies from Virginia City in 1887. Italians came to the state in the 1850s right after the Comstock Lode discovery. They worked in the mines (mainly gold and silver) and in the support industries as charcoal burners and mule packers.

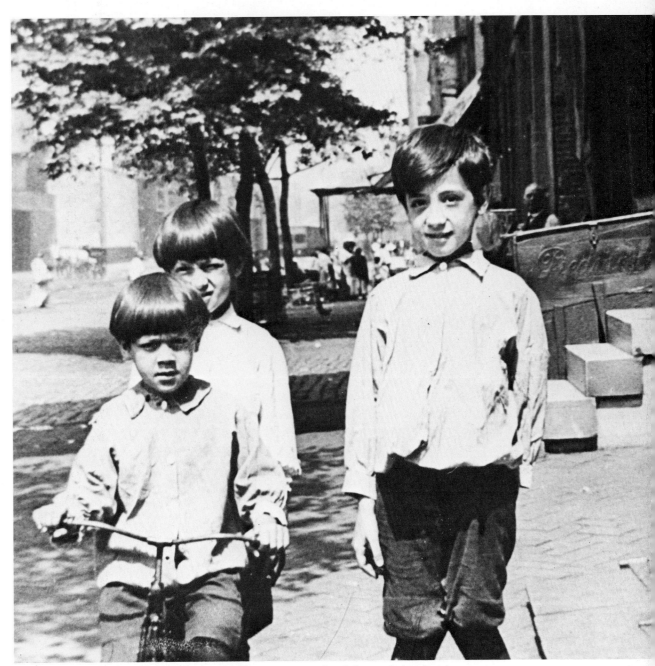

67. South Philadelphia. Dominic Sammartino sits on his bike with his brothers
Fred (behind) and Nicholas (right) in front of their home at 833 Washington
Avenue, Philadelphia, in 1918. In the background are people shopping at the
9th Street Italian curb markets. Across the street was Bryant's coal yard,
showing the mixture of residential and commercial properties that was typical
of most working-class sections in the early twentieth century.

Opposite:
66. Chicago immigrants. These Italian
Americans in the Hull House area of
Chicago sit amid the urban blight that
permeated the struggle for survival in
America.

68. Bocce. The Romans' game of bocce passed down through the centuries and found a home wherever Italians gathered. This court is in Tacoma, Washington.

69. Baking bread. Filomena (D'Aloia) and Luciano Cocchiarella remove bread baked in the earthen oven behind their home on Hopkins Street in St. Paul, Minnesota, in 1940. In other Italian communities some families would make their own bread dough and use the brick ovens of the local bakeries.

70. Growing tomatoes. Use of the land to supplement income and the pleasure of cultivating a garden that belonged to the family characterized Italian immigrant settlements. This Italian-Canadian family in Toronto sorts tomatoes grown behind their home.

71. Carting produce. Italian peddlers drive their wagons from the produce markets through the Italian section of Tacoma, Washington. Note the grape vines growing in the front yards.

72. The Italian Club at Thurber, Texas. Italians who settled in Thurber organized this club, shown here at a picnic. Many of the men in this picture worked in the mines owned by the Texas Pacific Coal Company.

73. Leapfrog. Children used the streets as playgrounds in the congested cities. Here they play leapfrog over a fire hydrant in New York City in 1911.

74. Baseball. This tenement alley in Boston, Massachusetts, in 1909 was converted into a playing field by the neighborhood children.

75. Roller coaster. Italian-American boys enjoy their homemade roller coaster in Cleveland, Ohio.

76. Baltimore saloon. Vincent Flaccomio owned this saloon on Forrest and Front streets in Baltimore, Maryland. (Close by is the Belair Market, where Italians operated fruit and vegetable stalls.) During the winter months the seasonally unemployed street laborers would gather to play cards and drink wine at Flaccomio's with their friends.

77. The Italian Sportsmens' Club. A 1926 banquet of the Italian American Sportsmen's Club Association of Trenton, New Jersey. A picture of King Umberto I of Italy is on the back wall.

78. Northwest Bocce Club. Players in the Northwest Bocce Club of Philadelphia in 1936 included Alfredo Cocozza, the future Mario Lanza.

79. Italian cowboys. Two Italian workers in Calgary, Canada, dressed as cowboys, which they called *banditi* when they sent this picture to their relatives back home.

80. The Columbus Circle Club. Organized in 1923 as a combination athletic and social club by the neighborhood boys in South Philadelphia, the club disbanded in 1927. Its successor, the Orioles Athletic Club, 1933–39, broke up as the "boys" got married.

Opposite:
81. Joe Roche. Virgil Aschero of San Francisco fought as Joe Roche in the middleweight division in the 1920s. Many Italian-American teenagers took up boxing in the hope that it would lead to fame and fortune. Roche is shown with his manager, Fred Winsor.

82. Joe Dundee. Italians in Tampa, Florida, feted Joe Dundee, the welterweight champion of the world, on tour in 1927. He is sitting to the right of the man with glasses in front of the piano.

83. Rocco Franco's music school. The Italians' love of music for home enjoyment supported Rocco Franco's music school in Chicago, Illinois. Franco taught violin, mandolin, and guitar.

ROCCO FRANCO

84. Italian bands. Maestro A. Quaranta organized and directed the Italian Royal Band of Pueblo, Colorado. Many of America's towns and cities recruited Italian musicians for their bands. In fact, some of the earliest immigrants were musicians recruited in 1805 from Italy by President Thomas Jefferson, who wanted to organize a brass band for the U.S. Marine Corps. In most cities Italian musicians dominated the municipal bands, forming Italian band associations that played at festivals and holiday celebrations.

85. Toronto's Italian Canadian Band.
During feasts the bands provided dance
music ranging from a tarantella to a fox-
trot. Bands also participated in funeral
processions, escorting the body from
home to the church.

86. Farfariello. A famous Italian
comedian born Eduardo Migliaccio,
Farfariello created character roles that
portrayed the immigrant experience. He
brought out the humor and the pathos
of the immigrant just arriving, the
laborer describing his *jobba*, and an
Italian woman dressed in regional
costume, describing life without her
husband, a sojourner in America.

87. Farfariello as an Italian-American soldier. Depicting a doughboy of World War I, Farfariello holds both countries' flags. He also caricatured the American who came into contact with the immigrants, such as the policeman equipped with a pipe and a nightstick.

88. Italian romance stories. A reading public required popular literature in Italian. Romance stories were offered in magazine form, as serializations in newspapers, and later dramatizations on Italian radio programs. These stories demonstrated the Italian-American adjustment to American styles of courtship and domestic life, as in *The Tragic Romance of Bianca of Larigliano* and *Woman Against Woman, A Passionate Romance of Love and Hate.*

89. Learning English. The children of immigrants struggled to learn English at school. Even American-born children entered school speaking only Italian. Children became interpreters and amanuenses for their foreign parents. Here "Pietro learns to write" on Jersey Street in New York.

Opposite:
90. Luisa Tetrazzini. Soprano Luisa Tetrazzini traveled from Rome, Italy, to San Francisco in 1914 to participate in the dedication of a statue to Giuseppe Verdi erected in Golden Gate Park.

71

91. Italian-American school. Education often separated English-speaking children from Italian-speaking parents, and intergenerational conflict sometimes resulted. In Ybor City, Tampa, Florida, at the turn of the century, Italian schools were organized that operated from a preschool level to approximately the third grade. Children learned the basics of reading, writing, and arithmetic in the Italian language. After completion of the third grade, most students changed over to the "American" public schools. The Tampa school also had an American teacher to teach English. She sits in the front to the left of Professor R. Scocozza.

Opposite:

93. Cleveland schoolyard during recess. For the immigrant, free education in America provided opportunities that were not available to all in Italy. Yet even though it was free, it was a luxury most families could not afford. Young children worked before or after school. They left school when they found permanent employment. Families made great sacrifices to keep their children in school, and there are many examples of lawyers and doctors who worked their way through school by tending bar in their father's saloon, shaving customers in their father's barbershop, or accepting financial help from older brothers and sisters.

92. Saluting the flag. American schools paid little attention to the cultural differences of their multiethnic students. The "melting pot" concept dominated education, and children were expected to embrace such American heroes as George Washington and Abraham Lincoln. Educational philosophy stressed modernity and conformity and succeeded in separating home and school. Here children salute the flag in a New York school in 1890.

94. Italian Mothercraft Class. The Board of Health in Toronto, Canada, in 1916 ran an Italian Mothercraft Class. An effort was made to wean mothers from their Old World customs that were considered unsanitary or even dangerous by "modern" scientific standards.

95. Settlement Houses. University-educated reformers brought their ideas of social justice and philosophical pragmatism into the immigrant sections of cities through the settlement houses. They lived in these houses and invited the neighborhood residents to use the building for educational and social activities. Here Italian men attend a citizenship class in Cleveland's Hiram House.

3
ENTERPRISE

96. A street huckster in Chicago. Fresh produce was brought to customers either in pushcarts, bushels carried on the shoulders, or by horse and wagon throughout America's cities. In many cities a connection developed between the businessmen who imported and distributed wholesale fruit and produce and the street peddlers who sold these items to local customers. A huckster who worked along the streets lined with middle- and upper-class homes often received gifts of discarded velvet curtains, porcelain-faced dolls, and somewhat faded doll carriages. This huckster is working on Chicago's Near West Side.

Most Italians came to America seeking work as a means to improve their family's condition in Italy. These migrants, overwhelmingly male, fanned out across America, taking jobs on railroad construction gangs, as street cleaners, ragpickers, miners, ditchdiggers, brick makers, stonemasons, peddlers, street musicians, and as workers in shops and factories. Many lived in boardinghouses or in bachelor quarters where expenses were kept to a minimum. These men expected to move when work was scarce or the weather too severe. Their impermanence was pronounced *gondolieri* (birds of passage) by the authorities and created a distance between them and the communities in which they worked. In time, some of these men moved out of the laboring class into enterprise. Peddlers opened produce stores, tailors set up their own custom shops, lodging houses became restaurants, and stonecutters fashioned monuments and statues.

At the same time, the size of the Italian community itself provided a market for ethnic business. Food importers, grocery stores, butchers, bakers, travel agents, and bankers catered to the particular needs and tastes of people who liked olive oil, goat's milk, and cannoli or those who needed help buying steamship tickets and sending money to relatives in Italy. A decision to remain in America encouraged economic expansion, such as real-estate investment and such business ventures as musical-instrument dealerships. Women began to emigrate to reunite their families in America. They earned money at a variety of jobs, ranging from crop harvesting to making artificial flowers. They also sold merchandise, cared for boarders, and helped their husbands and brothers operate retail businesses and service industries.

Some immigrants arrived in America with specific skills and capital that attracted the patronage of Americans. These men offered the fancy goods desired by middle- and upper-class Americans, such as notions, cameos, decorative ironwork, stone carving, and hairdressing. Most of these immigrants came to America either to advance their standard of living, for adventure, or in response to Italian political conditions or family disagreements. The very nature of their occupations and their small numbers in the Italian community contributed to their marginality as Italians. They might relate more to Americans than to the growing number of sojourners and settlers who worked and lived among conationals.

97. Shining shoes. Street trades and services expanded as thousands of Italian male immigrants between the ages of twelve and forty-five arrived in America in the late nineteenth century. Both the native and immigrant population benefited from itinerant workers like twelve-year-old Michael Mero from 2 West Fourth Street, Wilmington, Delaware, who shined shoes six hours a day in 1910.

98. Selling bread. On Mulberry Bend in New York City's Little Italy, a young boy sells Italian bread to a *paesana*. (The bread was probably day-old bakery goods.)

99. Hurdy-gurdy. Used by Antonio Vivaldi in one of his compositions, the hurdy-gurdy brought music into the streets of the New World. Typically, a man pushed the heavy machine balanced on two wheels, but these women in Toronto, Canada, cooperated in this enterprise. Organ-grinders strapped the instrument on their backs and hurdy-gurdy players used the tunes popular in America of that day.

100. Collecting trash. Italian laborers obtained jobs such as garbage collecting, helping to improve and civilize the atmosphere and appearance of American cities. Here at the corner of Christian and 10th, two workers collect trash in front of South Philadelphia's Fabiani Italian Hospital.

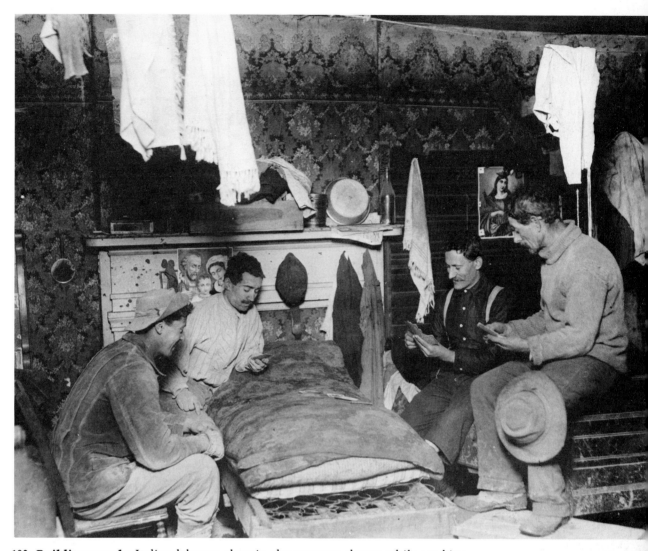

102. Building canals. Italian laborers slept in the quarters shown while working on the New York Barge Canal. When the company did not provide housing, *paesani* did. Other groups of men lived in boxcars and pooled their resources to pay for food.

Opposite:
101. Selling peanuts. Joseph Severio, an eleven-year-old peanut vendor in Wilmington, Delaware, in 1910, began selling peanuts at age nine, working six hours a day and giving all of his earnings to his father.

103. Building railroads. This *Pensione Italiana* in Price, Utah, was owned by Joe Bonacci, a section gang foreman on the Denver and Rio Grande Western Railroad. The *pensione*, or rooming house, was located behind the railroad depot.

104. Banking and labor center. Work was essential for the immigrant. He learned of opportunities from *paesani* and relatives or used the services of *padrones* (labor bosses working as employment agents for contractors, mine owners, railroad companies, and factories). Some of the more successful employment agents established offices in major cities. This bank and labor center was in New York.

105. Arizona boardinghouse. When wives, sisters, and mothers crossed the ocean to join their husbands, the homes they helped establish often provided male boarders with the Italian *ambiente* they missed. Here in the mining town of Morenci, Arizona, the boarders join the family in a 1907 picture of domestic harmony. Later the wife would wash their clothes and use the clothesline on the porch to dry them.

106. Construction work. Before coming to North America, Italian men had traveled outside of their cities and villages to other areas of Italy, Europe, North Africa, South America, and Australia where they used their construction skills for industrial projects. These men are grading and paving streets in Williamson, West Virginia, for the Pietro Paving & Construction Company of Morgantown.

107. Stonemasonry. Italian stonemasons work on Eastern Avenue in Toronto, Canada, in 1916. The expanding cities of North America required some of the building skills learned in Italy, and many immigrants were artisans who had worked at carpentry, stonecutting, bricklaying, and ironworking in their villages in Italy.

108. Textile mill. Workers build the New Worsted Mill in Lawrence, Massachusetts, in 1910. These mills produced a large percentage of woolen cloth in the world market. Italians, Poles, French Canadians, and others produced the fabric. It was here in 1912 that the famous Lawrence Strike took place over wage cuts.

109. Mining. Italian immigrants joined other ethnic workers in mines across the country. These men are working at the Bunker Hill Mine in Coeur d'Alene, Idaho. Italians participated in many of the violent strikes that occurred throughout the mining regions of America.

110. Blacksmithing. In mining communities blacksmiths cared for the horses used to pull the coal carts from the mines. Here blacksmith Peter Dalessandro shoes a horse in Luxor, Pennsylvania, about 1900.

111. Dock workers. Immigrants worked on the docks of Cleveland's Lake Front. The ore transported here from Michigan's iron range, where Italian miners worked, supplied the steel mills of Cleveland.

112. Fishing. Antonio Milietello and Vito Cannela are second-generation Americans living in the fishing town of Gloucester, Massachusetts. They are repairing a seining net belonging to their boat.

113. Picking strawberries. Italian agriculturists were highly prized by American land developers. In 1908 Hugh McRae, a realtor from Wilmington, North Carolina, established this St. Helena farm community for Italians. Other Italian farm communities were established in Independence, Louisiana; Vineland, New Jersey; and San Jose, California. Italians often worked their way up from migrant worker to tenant farmer to truck farm proprietor.

114. Dairy farming. Salvatore Reina sits on a stallion and Castenzio Ferlita stands holding the white horse on their dairy farm in Tampa, Florida, around 1894. They arrived in 1886 and in less than ten years ran this successful business. Later they established the Cosmopolitan Ice Company and the Tropical Ice Cream Company.

115. Del Monte foods. The Del Monte Canners Association produced the fruit and vegetables for the company. Here the members leave San Francisco for a picnic in 1907. Paul and Domenic Gallette are in the foreground.

116. Processing asparagus. These women, children of immigrants, were transported on trucks in 1940 from Trenton, New Jersey, to Morrisville, Pennsylvania, where they picked, graded, and bunched asparagus in a shed on Starkey Farms.

117. Fruit farming. Three generations of the Battaglia family work on their 30-acre fruit farm in California. They are sorting apricots for delivery to the local market in San Jose.

118. Coffee sweepings. At the turn of the century, many industries operated in homes. Immigrant families, including young children, worked long hours for low pay. Here Italian workers pick coffee sweepings in New York City. Each sack of sweepings cost 25 cents at the warehouse and the picked-over coffee sold at about 12 cents a pound.

119. Artificial flowers. Italian Americans worked in the small, crowded rooms where they lived—transforming their kitchens into workshops. Here the Ceru family makes flowers in their attic apartment at 143 Thompson Street, New York City.

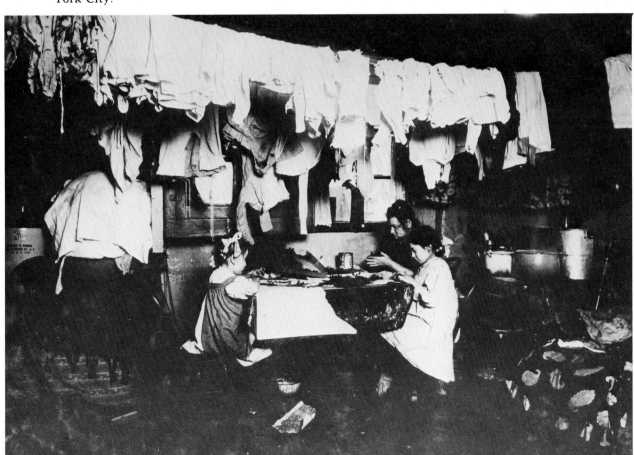

120. "Garment district." This row of tenements, 260 to 268 Elizabeth Street in New York, was typical of the housing environment of the immigrant workers who finished clothes at home.

121. Finishing clothes. This family on Hanover Street in Boston, Massachusetts, finishes garments for the subcontractor. Women learned about these jobs from neighbors and relatives or shop owners who would ask the proprietors of a grocery store if they knew of any women interested in working. In this family the children not only helped their mother, but also picked up and delivered the garments to the shop.

122. Making doll clothes. The Romana family makes dresses for Campbell Kid Dolls in their home at 59 Thompson Street, New York. Mrs. Romana's twelve-year-old son operated the sewing machine when his mother was not using it. But when she did use it, he busied himself by helping the younger children, ages five and seven, break threads.

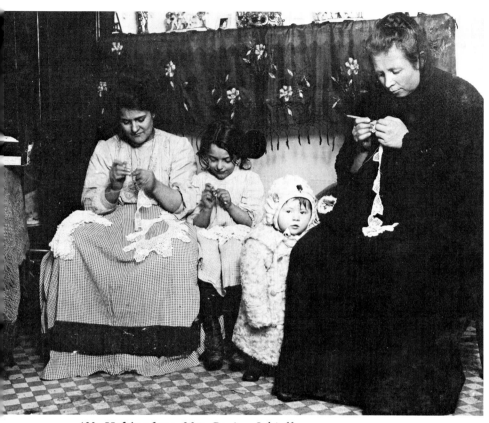

123. Making lace. Mrs. Rosina Schiaffo was a lace contractor for the M. Weber Company. In her apartment at 301 East 114th Street, she collected the work done by women in the neighborhood and taught newcomers how to make lace, providing a training program for the young and unskilled. Children were given needles and taught to sew at an early age. Many "graduated" at age thirteen or fourteen and went to work in factories, producing articles similar to the ones they had made at home.

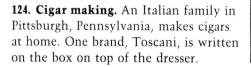

124. Cigar making. An Italian family in Pittsburgh, Pennsylvania, makes cigars at home. One brand, Toscani, is written on the box on top of the dresser.

100

125. Making handbags. The Caruso girls—ages six, nine, and eleven—work on making chain handbags at home, 32 Knight Street, Providence, Rhode Island. The debilitating effect of home work on the family attracted the attention of reformers who described the unsanitary, crowded conditions in which the manufacturing occurred and the toll it took on the lives and education of young children.

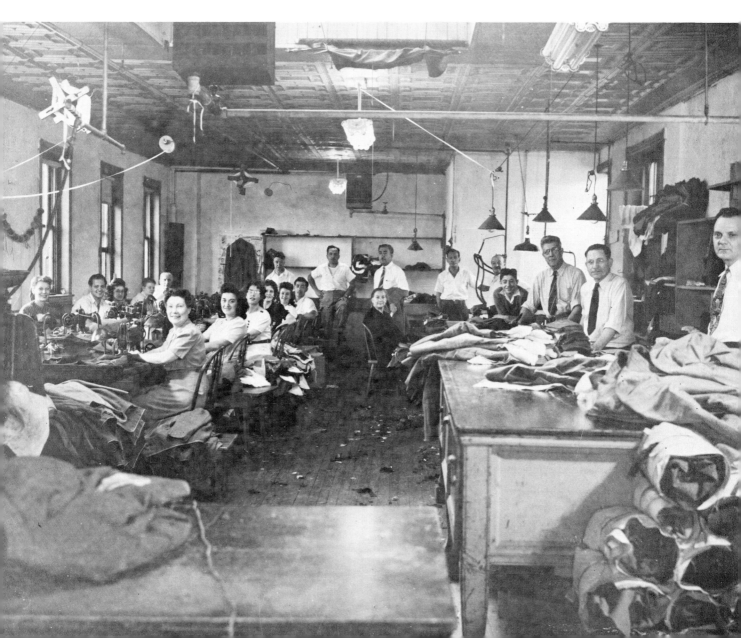

127. Making women's clothing. Italians settled in Wind Gap, Pennsylvania, because of work available in the slate quarries. Around World War I, small women's clothing shops were established in the area, and most of the owners, as well as the employees, were Italian Americans. This shop is Valerie Fashions, owned by Joseph Dell'Alba.

Opposite:
126. Making men's clothing. Antonio Apicella's men's clothing shop at Exeter and Gay streets in Baltimore, Maryland, employed East European as well as Italian workers in 1948. Apicella worked in a tailor shop before he went into partnership as a subcontractor.

128. Glassmaking. Greeks and blacks worked with Italians in the Cumberland Glass Works in Bridgeton, New Jersey. Many workers in this company had no previous Old World experience in this trade, even though glassmaking still remains an Italian art.

129. Pharmaceutical manufacturing. Italian women in Detroit found employment in drug companies. Here workers sort pills at Parke Davis.

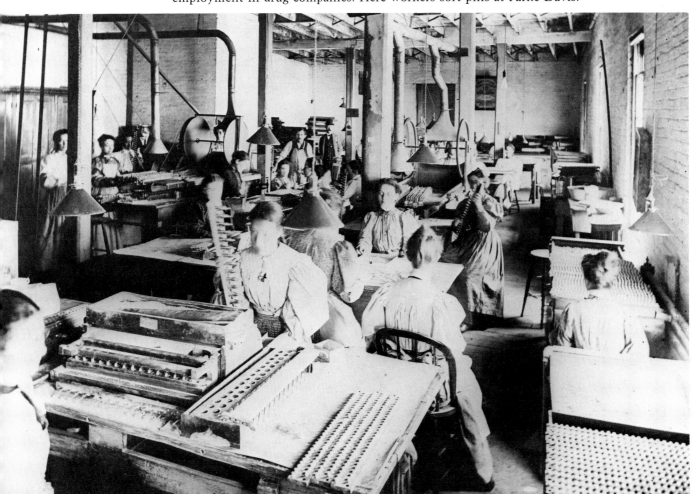

130. Sausage making. The Buon Gusto Sausage Factory used an Italian work force to supply the San Francisco area with Italian meat products in the 1920s.

105

131. Wine making. Louis Finocchiaro's winery and bottling works in Omaha, Nebraska, is an example of an Italian custom that continued in America. As the Italian population increased, a market developed for the products favored in the Italian diet.

132. Pasta making. Workers at the Piccolo Pete Macaroni Company in Omaha, Nebraska, in 1940.

133. Entrepreneur. Rocco Gualtieri combined the services of a bank, employment agency, ticket office, and grocery store in this building in Rome, New York. This center in the Italian community in the early decades of the twentieth century provided an opportunity for job recruitment and advertising. Men could purchase tickets at Gualtieri's to travel to work in other cities. They could also send part of their earnings back to their families, or buy steamship tickets to send to relatives wishing to emigrate to America.

134. Family business. The Porto Rico saloon, hotel, and grocery store in Albuquerque, New Mexico, was started in the 1890s by Frediano Alessandri, who emigrated from Italy after declaring bankruptcy. When Alessandri died in 1902, his nephew Alessandro Matteucci from Lammari, Lucca, operated the business. Matteucci had emigrated to America in 1896, joining his cousin Carlo Matteucci, who was employed by the Union Pacific Railroad in Winnemucca, Nevada. In turn, Alessandro sent for his brothers, each of whom operated businesses in Albuquerque, New Mexico.

135. Grocery store. Ida LaFata sits outside the grocery store in Detroit, Michigan, which her father, John, operated with his brother-in-law Sam Mercurio. As a child Ida operated the "penny candy department," a small, glassed-in case near the front of the store. She had to keep the glass bowls and trays clean and filled with a variety of candies.

136. Fruit importing. Salvatore Di Giorgio established a fruit-importing company in Baltimore, Maryland, in the 1890s. This picture of the first company truck dates back to 1904. Di Giorgio, like other immigrants from Cefalu, Sicily, specialized in fresh fruit and produce. In the 1920s he expanded his holdings to Florida and to California and later moved his business to the West Coast, where it grew into a multimillion-dollar corporation.

137. Imported tomatoes. Luigi Vitelli operated a company that imported products canned under his label in Italy and distributed them throughout the United States. These peeled tomatoes come from a location near Naples.

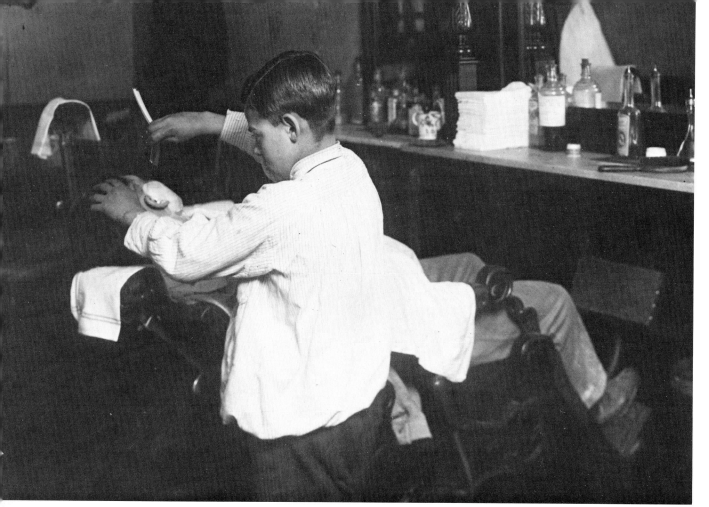

138. Barbershop. Frank De Natale, age twelve, works on a customer in his father's barbershop on Hanover Street in Boston. Italian fathers continued to teach their sons the trade they had learned before emigrating. Family apprenticeship provided help in the business and ensured that the business would be a legacy to pass on to the next generation.

139. Shoe mending. An Italian shoe mender in Omaha, Nebraska, in 1940. Artisans who were makers of shoes accommodated to the machine-produced products in America by offering repair services.

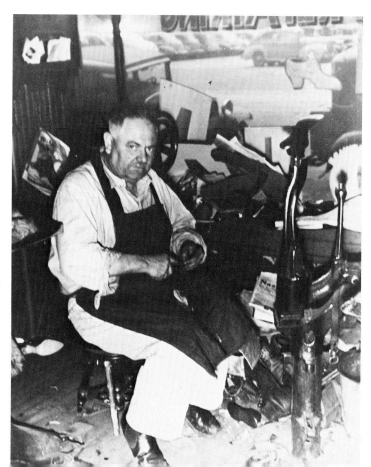

140. Bank and bar. In 1893 Liccione-Pittaro & Company ran a combination bank and bar on the corner of Hester and Mulberry streets in New York City. Men gathered together after work and on days off to share a glass of wine and play cards.

141. Tending bar. Regina Pozza from Buscato, Lombardy, stands behind her bar in St. Louis, Missouri. She and her husband established their business in 1919. After her husband's death in 1936, she continued to manage the family business until 1975.

142. Delivering bread. The N. Orlando Bakery, of Cleveland, Ohio, in 1936, and two of their delivery trucks.

143. Architecture. The well-known Italian architect Garbo designed and constructed many of Cleveland's commercial buildings. This picture of the Fountain Theatre illustrates the artwork that added beauty to a functional design.

144. Hotel and restaurant. At Fitzwater and Seventh streets in Philadelphia, Giannini's Hotel and Restaurant catered to the tastes of the South Philadelphia population.

145. Undertaker. Tomasso Scarpaci established this combination real-estate office and undertaker's establishment at 186 East 21st Street, Brooklyn, New York, around 1910. In the early part of the century, undertakers only embalmed the body and wakes were held in the home of the deceased.

146. Violin making. Italian immigrants with special skills found patrons in America who desired quality products. The A. F. Moglie Company sold old violins and manufactured new ones.

147. Stoneworkers. An Italian stoneworker in Omaha, Nebraska, in 1940. Many monuments in the United States include statues sculpted by Italian artists. For example, the first monument dedicated to President George Washington was erected in Baltimore, Maryland, and sculpted by Enrico Causici.

148. Bookstore. The Cavalli building and bookstore in its 1903 location on Columbus Avenue in San Francisco.

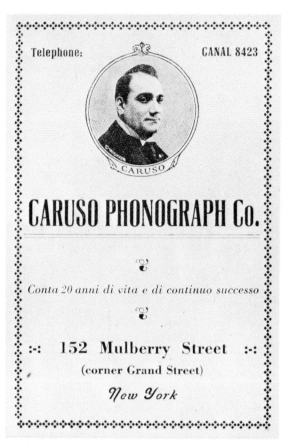

149. Phonograph manufacture. Enrico Caruso lent his name to this phonograph company located at Mulberry and Grand streets in New York. The company was established in 1905.

150. *L'Unione.* Italian-American newspapers were printed within reach of a large reading population. All the major cities supported these publications that combined news of Italy with news of Italian-American communities. Shown here is the staff of *L'Unione,* which was published in Pueblo, Colorado.

151. *Il Progresso.* The Italian press served the community in many ways. This picture was taken in front of New York City's *Il Progresso* in 1909 during a campaign the paper sponsored for relief of the victims of the Messina, Sicily, earthquake of December 1908.

4

PREJUDICE, VIOLENCE, RADICALISM, AND UNIONISM

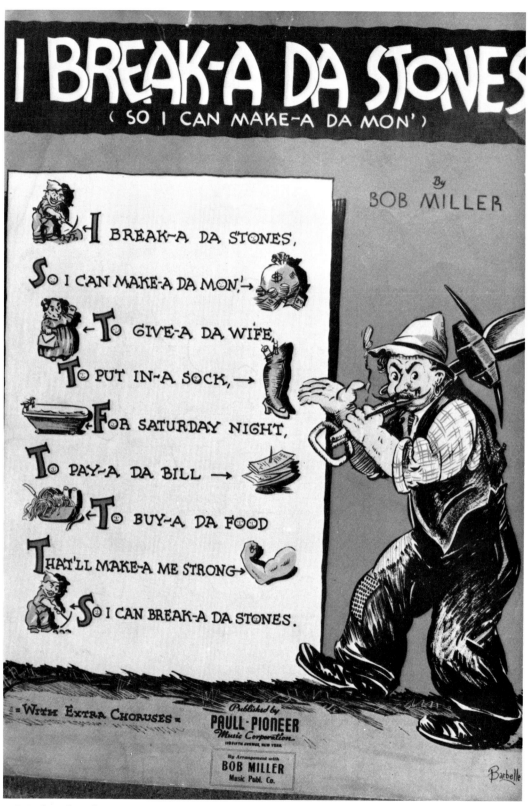

152. "I break-a da stones." American humor capitalized on the image of the ill-educated immigrant worker whose lack of English and lack of job skills forced him to become a street laborer, as depicted by this sheet music. Americans considered the low-paying, back-breaking jobs distasteful and they laughed at the men who were willing to accept them.

From the 1880s on, thousands of Italians crossed the ocean each year to help build and refine a growing nation. Fortunately, this mass migration coincided with North America's industrial development and expansion during the late nineteenth century. These southern Italian newcomers were more visible to the Americans than the northern Italians who arrived earlier in the century. They came in large numbers, settled in urban or industrial areas, and most were poor, many illiterate. Their strange customs, including their adherence to Roman Catholicism, frightened Americans.

As America's cities grew, an increase in the crime rate, the deterioration of housing, and manipulation of the political process accelerated. Most Americans blamed these changes on the foreign element. The existence of crime among the immigrants, the negative image of the *padrone*, or boss, and the radical political beliefs of some newcomers contributed to the suspicions and prejudices held by many Americans. The American press attracted readership by writing lurid accounts of Black Hand activities. The kidnappings, extortions, thefts, and killings attributed to this criminal element were usually restricted within the immigrant community, but whenever crime involved the native population, such as the assassination of New Orleans' Police Chief David Hennessy in 1890, the public overreacted. In this instance hundreds of Italians were arrested, and many were ill-treated by the authorities. When eight men were tried and acquitted because the jury did not deliver a sentence, angry citizens organized a protest rally. The leaders, prominent men in the community, advocated vengeance. The crowd turned into a mob, took up arms, broke into the parish prison, and lynched eleven Italians. The Italian government protested, recalled its ambassador from the United States, and the possibility of war figured in congressional debates. The United States government eventually paid indemnities to the families of the murdered prisoners, but Louisiana authorities failed to prosecute anyone involved in the lynchings.

Other negative images of Italians included the street musicians, mainly organ-grinders who "disturbed" the quiet, residential tone of middle- and upper-class neighborhoods, and the *padrone* who supplied immigrant labor and sometimes votes. While the organ-grinder's appearance and music were unpleasant to some Americans, the *padrone* was seen as the symbol of foreign corruption brought to American shores. American workers were convinced that *padroni* imported men who would flood the labor pool and decrease wages. American authorities condemned the practices of unscrupulous bosses who exploited these immigrant workers by charging them a fee for obtaining a job (while also collecting payment from the employer), overcharging them for transportation to the job and for room and board on the job site, and exacting high interest rates for money loaned to them. Official accounts of such criminal practices made the word *padrone* synonymous with *thief* or *felon*. Yet not all *padroni* exploited workers. Many served as employment agents, channeling job seekers to work opportunities. They profited as businessmen who provided services needed by the immigrant worker, and they were regarded as community leaders.

A rapidly changing society that was subject to unpredictable economic cycles and social maladjustments often found a release for its confusion and frustration in anti-immigrant sentiments. The Italians' recreation out of doors and their extroverted daily life; their eating habits, including foods strange to the American palate, such as garlic, spices, snails; their public practice of Catholicism replete with feasts and processions—all this separated them from a society that followed Anglo-Saxon-Protestant values. Efforts to restrict immigration, especially from southern and eastern Europe, grew in intensity as the number of newcomers increased and as Americans became convinced that the foreigners threatened to undermine American democracy and Protestantism and to cause economic chaos.

Americans also responded negatively to the violence that characterized many labor disputes during the late nineteenth and early twentieth centuries. Foreign radicals were blamed for the Haymarket Riot of 1886 and a series of strikes that occurred throughout the nation. Some immigrants were committed to political and economic philosophies that questioned the values of the American political system and capitalism. Their alternatives ranged from socialism to communism, syndicalism, and anarchism. They represented a small portion of the mass migration, but, when united with American radicals, they seemed a real and present danger to the established system.

Italian radicals contributed to the development of class consciousness among their conationals as well as other workers. Their speeches, writings, and group actions highlighted the struggle for social justice. Some of America's leaders of organized labor came out of this heritage of alternative philosophies. They adapted their beliefs to the realities of American capitalism and forged organizations to protect factory and industrial workers. The Lawrence, Massachusetts, strikes of 1912 and 1919 are only two examples of Italian-American radical activity that provided strike tactics and worker cooperation. Unions, such as the International Ladies Garment Workers Union and the Amalgamated Clothing Workers of America, benefited from the leadership of Italian organizers and the support of Italian-American union members.

For the Italian-American worker, unionism was one way of protesting the poor working conditions of industrial America. They also fought against unfair treatment in federal legislation, which proposed literacy as a requirement for admission to America, and state legislation that discriminated against foreigners. They protested against the stereotypes that characterized Italians as stupid buffoons or sly criminals. The conviction of Sacco and Vanzetti and their seven years of frustrating appeals served as evidence to many that Americans despised Italians.

The majority of immigrants who made America their home worked hard at becoming a part of their adopted country. They participated in the major activities of American society and incorporated its values. Although they remained aware of the events taking place and of the conditions back in the land of their birth, they were concerned about their immediate world. As Americans, they responded to the call to arms in World War I and World War II, they cheered the Allied victory, sold war bonds, and supported the belief that the preservation of democracy was an important part of their heritage.

During the interwar years, the rise to power of Benito Mussolini in Italy introduced a new dimension in Italian-American communities. Many immigrants believed that his government would benefit the Italian people, their relatives, and friends; and many immigrants read the glowing accounts of Il Duce written in the 1920s by American journalists, philosophers, and politicians. By the early 1930s, the New Deal program of Franklin D. Roosevelt echoed some of the programs introduced by Mussolini, and many Americans believed that the United States would benefit from strong leadership—fascist style. For some immigrants, Mussolini's overseas expansion into Abyssinia, Ethiopia, and Somaliland meant that Italy—and, as a result, all Italians—gained the respect and admiration of the powerful nations. Italian-American pride in and support of Italy in the 1930s was more a reaffirmation of their ethnic identity and the need for recognition than an endorsement of the actual form of government and tactics of Mussolini. They were happy to see the emergence of Italy as a world power, but their loyalty to America was stronger. The same men and women who sent their gold rings to Il Duce in 1935 proudly sent off their sons to the armed forces of Canada and the United States in 1940 and 1941: The immigrants had chosen.

Their choice to become Americans incorporated their Italian identity. Across America the celebration of Columbus Day, a reminder that an Italian discovered the New World, and that it was named for another, Amerigo Vespucci, demonstrated pride in their dual heritage.

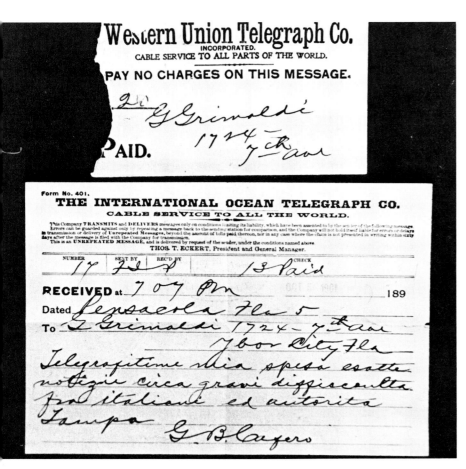

153. Trouble in Tampa. The Italian government attempted to protect immigrants from the more obvious forms of injustice. When the Italian consul in Pensacola, Florida, heard about the trouble in Tampa between the authorities and the Italians, he cabled for information: "Send me a telegram at my expense, explaining about the grave difficulties between the Italians and the authorities in Tampa." Rumors abounded that armed Italians would storm the Tampa city hall to protest the wholesale arrest of striking cigar workers. A vigilante group rushed into Ybor City to stop the plan and were amazed to find that the group were Italian women—the wives and sisters of the arrested strikers.

154. Sacco and Vanzetti. The trial of Nicola Sacco and Bartolomeo Vanzetti in 1920–21 focused attention on the plight of Italian immigrants suspected of holding dangerous beliefs. Their conviction for the murder of a payroll guard in Massachusetts was challenged by those who questioned the impartiality of American justice. Judge Webster Thayer's behavior during their trial convinced many people that they were condemned because of their anarchist philosophy and alien status. This commemorative card contains a quotation in which Sacco indicts Thayer for persecuting, terrorizing, and killing the people. He and Vanzetti were electrocuted in August 1927 after 124 all appeals were denied.

NICOLA SACCO
(Al giudice Thayer, 9 Aprile 1927):

VOI perseguitate il popolo, lo terrorizzate, l'uccidete. NOI l'educhiamo, lo risvegliamo. Ecco perché oggi siamo qui e VOI lo sapete, giudice, perché io muoio. Lo sapevate ieri, lo saprete domani e sempre che NOI non siamo colpevoli.

(Condannato alla sedia elettrica, come nel 1920).

155. Prohibition. During Prohibition, 1919 to 1933, many Americans ignored or violated the law. Demand for alcohol increased, and people willing to risk arrest profited from the sale and manufacture of liquor. Italians had brought to America a culture that linked moderate drinking with daily life. They continued to make wine, and some branched out into making beer and whiskey that they sold to many of their communities' leading citizens. Law officials attempted to enforce the law and are shown here destroying a still in St. Louis' Hill district.

156. Fighting crime. While many Americans suspected all Sicilians, Calabrians, and Neapolitans of belonging to or aiding the criminal "mafia" organizations, they remained indifferent to the efforts of Italian Americans to eliminate crime from their own communities. Italian detective Charles Carola receives a gold badge in 1915 in appreciation of his success in breaking up an Italian gang in Cleveland, Ohio.

157. Lawrence Strike. Italian immigrants demonstrating for higher wages and better working conditions met opposition from corporation owners and law officials. In 1912 Lawrence, Massachusetts, was the scene of a major strike in the textile industry. The police attempted to stop the strikers from demonstrating in the streets by arresting such people as this Italian-American girl.

158. Industrial Workers of the World. During the Lawrence Strike two Italian
leaders, Joseph Ettor and Arturo Giovannitti, were arrested for creating the
disturbance that caused the death of an Italian-American female striker.
Authorities hoped that the arrest of the two organizers for the syndicalist
Industrial Workers of the World would defuse the strike. Instead, strikers of
many nationalities rallied to their cause. Here strikers hold IWW papers printed
in different languages. Joseph Ettor looks out from behind a tree.

159. Strike in New Jersey. The children of striking workers in the silk mills of Paterson, New Jersey, dramatize their parents' cause by participating in a May Day parade in New York City, 1913. Many Italians worked in the mills. Continuing a practice developed in Italy, striking workers often sent their children to safety in other communities.

160. Strike in New York. Italian and Jewish garment workers demonstrate in New York's Union Square in 1913. The Italian signs call for union shops and the end of spies and paid informers of the bosses. At that time immigrants constituted 75 percent of the workers in America's clothing industry. From the ranks of the Italian workers came such early union leaders as Luigi Antonini of the International Ladies Garment Workers Union and Frank Bellanca of the Amalgamated Clothing Workers of America.

161. Strike in Utah. Striking Italian miners in Utah sought refuge in Paul and Barbara Pessetto's "Halfway House" (halfway between Castle Gate and Helper, Utah) in 1903. The Pessettos were arrested during the United Mine Workers of America's strike of 1903–04.

162. Strike demonstration. Demonstrators in New York City protested the arrest of Italian anarchist Carlo Tresca during the iron ore miners' strike in Hibbing, Minnesota, in 1916.

163. Strike in Michigan. In Calumet, Michigan, in 1913, a false fire alarm that was set during a gathering of striking workers in the Italian hall on Christmas Eve resulted in a panic in which people were killed by the frightened crowd. The entire community in this copper-mining district attended the funeral of the victims.

164. Death of a labor leader. The funeral cortege of Joe Hill, the famous labor organizer, as it passes through an Italian section in Chicago in 1915. Many Italian socialists supported and sympathized with the beliefs of "American" activists, such as Joe Hill and Eugene V. Debs.

165. Ladies Garment Workers Union.
Angela Bambace began work in an East Harlem shirtwaist factory in 1917. She and her sister Marie protested against low wages and inadequate working conditions. Their success in organizing Italian women workers during the 1919 strike was appreciated by the officials of the International Ladies Garment Workers Union. In 1934 David Dubinsky sent Angela to Baltimore to organize factory workers there. Her successful efforts expanded union membership in Maryland, Virginia, and West Virginia. In 1956 she became the first and only Italian-American woman elected vice-president of the ILGWU.

166. Call for a strike. Organized labor joined all workers together in the fight for social justice. This poster, printed in Lithuanian, English, Italian, and Yiddish, urges workers in Philadelphia's garment industry to participate in a general strike during the 1920s.

167. Strike in Pennsylvania. In 1938 Italian and black American agricultural workers in Morrisville, Pennsylvania, went on strike in order to obtain wages higher than the 17 to 20 cents per hour they received and to protest their crowded, substandard housing conditions.

168. Italian Socialist Party of America. Some Italian immigrants brought with them economic and political ideas about the role of government and the importance of the working class. This 1926 cover of the Italian Socialist Party of America's publication illustrates its belief that basic industries should be owned by the state for the people.

169. Socialist Labor Party. The Italian section of the Socialist Labor Party in Hallowell, Maine, in 1898 spent a Sunday afternoon discussing the articles in *Il Guido del Popolo* (*A Guide for the People*) and *Lotte di Classe* (*Class Struggle*). They condemned the institution of capitalism as being exploitative of the workers who produced the goods for society.

170. Anarchists did not support any type of organization. This East Boston publication of 1913, *Gruppo Autonomo* (or *Autonomous Group*), lampoons the American political system by showing how elected officials are controlled by capitalists.

171. Lorenzo Panepinto. The Sicilian anarchist Lorenzo Panepinto (seated on far right) attempted to educate immigrants in Ybor City, Tampa, Florida, between 1909 and 1910. He organized and taught in the first Italian school and also shared his political beliefs with these members of a political club. Many of Tampa's Italians were active in the labor struggles in the cigar industry. They also expressed their political involvement by contributing to the Cuban revolutionaries of the 1890s.

172. Help for earthquake victims. Italian immigrants remained concerned with their friends and relatives still in Italy. In January 1909 New York City's Italians gave money and clothing for the relief of the victims of the Messina earthquake. Here people toss their contributions from their tenement windows to collectors standing with horses and carriages on the street below.

173. Off to war. In 1915 Italy joined France, England, and Russia against the Central Powers. Some immigrants returned to Italy to serve in the war, while others in 1917 enlisted or were drafted into the American Army. Here Italian-American soldiers in Tampa, Florida, pose with the U.S. and Italian flags.

174. Italian Red Cross. Italian-American organizations and the Italian consulate in New Orleans sponsored an annual fund-raising event for the Italian Red Cross during World War I. Here Red Cross volunteers pose at the fairgrounds.

175. End of the war. Italian Americans in St. Paul, Minnesota, participate in a parade celebrating the end of World War I. The girls on the float are wearing Italian peasant costumes.

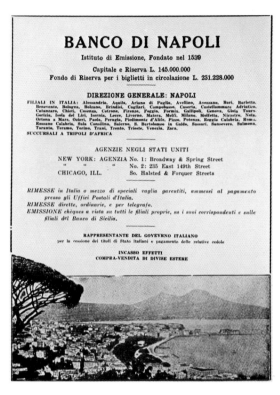

BANCO DI NAPOLI

Istituto di Emissione, Fondato nel 1539

Capitale e Riserva L. 145.000.000
Fondo di Riserva per i biglietti in circolazione L. 231.228.000

DIREZIONE GENERALE: NAPOLI

FILIALI IN ITALIA: Alessandria, Aquila, Ariano di Puglia, Avellino, Avezzano, Bari, Barletta, Benevento, Bologna, Bolzano, Brindisi, Cagliari, Campobasso, Caserta, Castellammare Adriatico, Catanzaro, Chieti, Cosenza, Cetrone, Firenze, Foggia, Formia, Gallipoli, Genova, Gioia Tauro, Gorizia, Isola del Liri, Isernia, Lecce, Livorno, Matera, Melfi, Milano, Molfetta, Nicastro, Nola, Ortona a Mare, Ozieri, Paola, Perugia, Piedimonte d'Alife, Pizzo, Potenza, Reggio Calabria, Roma, Rossano Calabria, Sala Consilina, Salerno, S. Bartolomeo in Galdo, Sassari, Sansevero, Sulmona, Taranto, Teramo, Torino, Trani, Trento, Trieste, Venezia, Zara.

SUCCURSALI A TRIPOLI D'AFRICA

AGENZIE NEGLI STATI UNITI

NEW YORK: AGENZIA No. 1: Broadway & Spring Street
"   "   No. 2: 235 East 149th Street
CHICAGO, ILL.   So. Halsted & Forquer Streets

RIMESSE in Italia a mezzo di speciali vaglia garentiti, ammessi al pagamento presso gli Uffici Postali d'Italia.
RIMESSE dirette, ordinarie, e per telegrafo.
EMISSIONE chèques a vista su tutti le filiali proprie, su i suoi corrispondenti e sulle filiali del Banco di Sicilia.

RAPPRESENTANTE DEL GOVERNO ITALIANO
per la cessione dei titoli di Stato Italiani e pagamento delle relative cedole

INCASSO EFFETTI
COMPRA-VENDITA DI DIVISE ESTERE

176. Banco di Napoli. The Italian government named the Banco di Napoli as official agent for the overseas immigrant community. Money could be exchanged or sent to relatives in Italy. Officials hoped to undermine private "bankers" who sometimes swindled illiterate immigrants who trusted them with their savings.

177. Conditions in America. Italian officials investigated the treatment and conditions of immigrants in America and condemned violence, exploitation, and discrimination. Reports warned prospective emigrants about these problems. Here a delegation headed by Fortunato Anselmo, the Italian vice-consul for Utah, visits Castle Gate after a mine explosion in 1924.

178. Italy-America Society. Interaction between Italy and America continued as the settlements of immigrants supported the representatives of Italy. This 1920 banquet of the Italy-America Society in New York honors the Italian Ambassador C. Romano Avezzana.

179. Welcoming Marconi. Baltimore's Italian-American community welcomes Italian physicist Guglielmo Marconi (inventor of a practical system of radiotelegraphy) in the 1930s. He holds the RCA Victor dog on a leash. Local leaders include Vincent Flaccomio, grand venerable of the Maryland Lodge of Sons of Italy in America; Placido Milio, travel-agency owner and agent of the Banco di Napoli (both stand to the left of the Italian Embassy military attaché); Vincent Palmisano, U.S. congressman; and Benjamin Apicella, banker and businessman (far right).

180. Welcoming General Diaz. Some Italian Americans were proud when some leading American political writers, journalists, and politicians during the 1920s and 1930s praised the economic development of fascism. Here Italian Americans of Cleveland welcome General Diaz on an official visit to the United States. He is accompanied by U.S. General Buckey and the Italian Consul Nicola Cerri.

181. Mussolini's government encouraged Italian immigrants to preserve their heritage and respect for their country of origin. He helped support the Dopo Scuola (After School) movement which established Italian language and social studies classes for second-generation children in American cities. Mrs. Octavia Benintende conducted this After School class in St. Philip's Elementary School in New Orleans' French Quarter around 1930.

182. Italy's need for gold in the 1930s to support its expanding economic and military ambitions prompted a campaign among immigrants to send gold wedding rings and jewelry to La Patria, the homeland. This photo illustrates the results of a collection from North Bay, Ontario, in 1936.

183. Celebrating Italy's victory. Italian Americans combined a celebration of the victory of Italy in World War I and the fifteenth anniversary of the Marcia su Roma of Mussolini in this 1936 procession of the Associazione Ex-Combattenti Italiano (veterans) in New Orleans' Audubon Park.

184. Decrying fascism. The rise of fascism created dissension in the North American Italian communities, and antifascists condemned the criminal acts of Mussolini's government. This front page article in a 1923 issue of *L'Unione* of Pueblo, Colorado, details the opposing view.

185. Italian Socialists in Chicago issued this broadside poster when the Italian military hero, Italo Balbo, visited the 1933 exposition there.

Who is Balbo?

MATTEOTTI

Balbo was instrumental in the killing of Giacomo Matteotti, the famous Italian Socialist deputy, who was murdered in cold blood because he dared to protest against the murder and oppression of Italian workers by Mussolini. Matteotti holds the same place in the hearts of Italians that Abraham Lincoln does in the hearts of all Americans.

Balbo congratulated and protected the murderers of the Rev. Don Minzoni, a Catholic priest of Argenta. The Papacy was outraged at this "Crime of Argenta," but now they have made peace with Mussolini and Cardinal Mundelein will celebrate mass for this protector of assassins.

Balbo was the director of many murders in province of Ferrara. His reputation as a terrorist was so bad at one time that he was removed as General of the fascist militia. When Balbo sued the "La Voce Repubblicana" for publishing the details of some of the above murders, he lost the suit. This even in fascist Italy!

It is a disgrace that this murderer and terrorist should be received by Democratic America as the official representative of the Italian people. This man no more represents the Italian people than Kaiser Wilhelm represented the German people. There should be no place in this free country for such tyrants.

This terrorism continues today and the Italian-born American workers protest against this infamy in the name of Matteotti and all our other murdered comrades. We ask American workers of all races to join us in protesting against the reception given to this murderer.

Italian Socialist Federation
Italian League for the Rights of Man

186. During World War II, Italians in North America supported the fight against Hitler and Mussolini. For the majority of immigrants, support for Mussolini had never extended to a loss of primary loyalty to America. In Buffalo, New York, Bessie Bellanca, a florist, used this painted Sicilian cart filled with flowers to promote the sale of war bonds.

187. The war effort. Mary Piasenti from Tiene, Italy, and Mary Guiliano from Foggia, Apulia, Italy, assemble generator equipment for bombers in an Oakland, California, defense plant. Their sons were fighting in the U.S. armed forces.

188. Prisoners of war. Paul Razzeca and Mike Falvo visit with two Italian prisoners of war in Magna, Utah, in 1944. Local Italian-American communities extended their hospitality to these men who shared their ethnic background. The ties were personal, not political. Many prisoners of war visited relatives living in America, and many Italian-American soldiers fighting in Italy renewed ties with family members still residing there.

189. Fighting Il Duce. Mr. and Mrs. Joseph Vita of Port Chester, New York, point to the spot in Italy where their U.S. soldier son, John, made a speech on Mussolini's balcony. John Vita used Il Duce's palace to tell the world what he and other Americans thought about fascism.

190. End of World War II. Residents of Baltimore's Little Italy raise a flag blessed and dedicated in 1942 to celebrate the end of World War II. The banner, which was hung across Eastern Avenue, displayed one star for each of the eighty-five young men who left for war in 1942.

191. Columbus Day in Florida. Each October Italian immigrants reminded Americans that it was the Italian explorer Christopher Columbus whose voyages initiated European settlement in the New World. Here in Tampa, Florida, around 1910 a group of Italian Americans dressed as sailors and Indians pose in front of a streetcar driven by the explorer Columbus.

192. Columbus Day in Detroit. Sam Mercurio and Joseph Cianciolo sit in the back seat of this decorated car in the 1911 Detroit Columbus Day parade. Mercurio's niece, Ida, and brother-in-law John LaFata stand on the running board.

193. Columbus Day in Colorado. C. F. Delliquadri rides a horse in Pueblo, Colorado's 1915 Columbus Day celebration. He served on the police force and was active in sponsoring the naturalization applications for many immigrants.

194. Honoring Columbus. Italian Americans gather on the state capitol grounds in St. Paul, Minnesota, in 1931 to dedicate a statue to Christopher Columbus. Elsewhere in America statues honoring the explorer were erected under the auspices of Italian-American organizations.

195. Italian Canadians in North Bay, Ontario, reminded their neighbors that the explorer John Cabot, who sailed to the area around Newfoundland in 1497, was born Giovanni Caboto. In the 1930s this North Bay drama group performed a play to raise money for a statue commemorating the Italian explorer.

5
RELIGION

Opposite:
196. St. Ambrose Church, St. Louis. In 1926 the second St. Ambrose Church was constructed by the Italian community on the Hill in southwest St. Louis, Missouri. When the original wooden-framed church established in 1903 burned down, the parishioners decided to model the new building after the church of San Ambrosio they attended in Milan. The facade of the 1926 structure shows the artistry of the skilled immigrant stonemasons and bricklayers who helped in the construction.

For Italians, the Roman Catholic church and their public devotion to God and the saints were almost inseparable from everyday life. Roman Catholicism was the established faith of the Italian nation, supported by the state, and most adhered to its teachings.

The history of Italy is rich in the variety of cultures and the beliefs that have influenced its people. The coming of Catholicism (Christianity) provided another way to worship and understand the supernatural. Many forms of worship combined characteristics of the Near Eastern religions with the new faith. The use of oil, the ceremony of baptism, and the belief in the transformation of bread and wine into the body and blood of Christ had parallels in other religions known to the Italians (Romans). Many people accepted their faith without a knowledge of theological explanations. The mysteries and drama of Christianity offered a way to express their concerns and questions about life.

For many Italian Catholics worship meant the personal bond between

157

the individual and his or her patron saint. Vows or promises were sealed with gifts of money or food, or activities such as fasting or other physical sacrifice. Celebrations of saints' days filled the calendar and each town and region had its own favorite devotions. Special societies were formed to aid in the annual celebration, which took on a festive atmosphere. The church was decorated with flowers, with statues adorned in rich clothing and candles ablaze. A procession was formed to carry the saint's image through the streets. Bands joined the procession, and the young men of the town carried the statue. Many devout worshipers walked barefoot as a penance or for a special vow.

Many of these traditions became part of the Italian-American experience. Yet it was difficult for the newcomers. By the time of the mass migration of Italians, the American Catholic church was dominated by Irish-American Catholics. These "native" American clergy were uncomfortable and embarrassed by the religious practices of the immigrants from southern and eastern Europe. They viewed the strange forms of worship as pagan and attempted to transform the newcomers into American Catholics.

The Americanization policy of the church hierarchy appeared discriminatory to the immigrants. Polish Catholics as well as Italian Catholics who wished to worship in their native language were assigned space in church basements. Most bishops fought requests to establish separate parishes or to assign immigrant priests to conational congregations. The persistence of ethnicity finally produced a compromise with the establishment of national parishes. These parishes did not have geographic (neighborhood) boundaries. Any person of that nationality could join the congregation. St. Mary Magdalen di Pazzi in Philadelphia and Saint Anthony di Padua of New York City and New Orleans were designated national parishes for the Italians before the Civil War. Italian immigrants joined together in initiating ethnic parishes. They collected funds, donated their labor, and built churches across America.

Special religious orders, like the Salesians, the Scalabrini, and the Congregation of the Missionary Sisters of the Sacred Heart, were founded in Italy to serve the Italian immigrants who settled throughout the world.

Not all Italians belonged to the Catholic church or practiced Catholicism. For some it was a matter of belief. The Waldenses of northern Italy had embraced Protestantism during the Reformation. A group of Waldenses founded Valdese, North Carolina, in 1893. During the nineteenth century, Protestant groups established missions in Italy. Some of their converts became ministers and were assigned to immigrant missions in American cities. Protestant missions in North American cities catered to the needs, physical and spiritual, of the immigrants. Methodist, Presbyterian, and Episcopal groups opened soup kitchens and dispensed clothing, food, and money to needy families. Their centers offered recreational and educational services for the community. Day schools, vacation schools, citizenship classes, and health-science classes attracted local residents. Most Italians who attended appreciated the kindness of the organizers, but saw no need to convert. The few who did participated fully in church activities, helping to construct buildings and attempting to convert their neighbors.

Proselytizing efforts reaped minimal results in America because Protestants misinterpreted Italian religious behavior. They assumed that the absence of men from church meant repudiation of the faith. But many Italians separated their religious devotion from church membership. They accepted their faith, but saw little need to attend mass or visit church. Their faith was a personal commitment expressed in devotions such as shrines at home, participation in saints' feasts, or special activities (for example, not eating wheat products on St. Lucy's Day—December 13—or making trips to religious shrines).

In America, as in Italy, organizations of lay people formed for the purpose of providing individual services and celebrating the feasts of patron saints. Societies such as the Società Italiana di Mutuo Beneficenza Maria Immacolata Concezione (established in 1904 in White Castle, Louisiana) provided sick and death benefits for its members, before the days of unemployment insurance and health-care programs, and coordinated the annual feast dedicated to the members' patron saint (the Blessed Mother). Not all groups incorporated both functions. The sole purpose of the Saint Gabriel Society of Baltimore, Maryland, for example, was to organize the annual feast held during the week of August 24.

Some immigrants had strong disagreements with the church. In Italy, the landowning church had exploited the *contadini*. Some local priests gave little of their time to the needs of the poorer congregants and viewed the priesthood as a means to gain social acceptance among the landowning classes. This "liaison" between the clergy and the landowners created resentment.

Also among the immigrants were individuals who did not accept church theology at all. These ranged from skeptics to anarchists. Their numbers were small, but in America they expressed themselves openly in the radical press and in organizations. These groups sometimes directly challenged the clergy and attempted to convince conationals that the church worked with the agents of exploitation, or at least represented obsolete, unscientific views.

The immigrant community gradually adopted American religious attitudes. Men, especially the second generation, attended mass and joined Holy Name societies. Clergy encouraged the establishment of activities and organizations to parallel those of the native Protestant society. Scout troops, church basketball teams, and mothers' clubs were established for parishioners.

Although the second and third generations formalized their participation in American church activities, they also retained some of the traditional forms of devotion. In New Orleans, the annual St. Joseph's Day parade (March 19) continues a devotion established by the immigrants. Each year in September, San Gennaro's feast in New York City attracts tourists who enjoy the food and festive atmosphere that accompanies the religious celebration.

197. Cleveland Italians built the foundations for San Rocco's Church on Fullerton Road. For many immigrants the donation of their labor represented the only way they could contribute to the cost of construction.

198. Livia Ardolino arrived in St. Paul, Minnesota, from Italy on December 7, 1920, and married Louis Pachiano at Holy Redeemer Church on December 9. She had become acquainted with and agreed to marry Louis via letters.

199. Baptism. Anthony Mercurio's 1918 baptism party pose outside his Detroit, Michigan, home. This household consisted of two families and included the grandparents.

200. A boy's First Communion portrait, Philadelphia, Pennsylvania, in the 1930s.

201. First Communion class poses with the pastor at St. Anthony's Church on Clinton Avenue in Hamilton, Ontario, Canada. For most immigrant and second-generation children religious education was taught after regular school hours. Parochial schools charged a nominal tuition, and working-class parents often decided to use the free, public-school system.

202. Confirmation. The sacrament of confirmation was symbolic of the transformation from childhood to adulthood. Confirmation meant that the individual was considered to be a ''soldier of Christ.'' For many Italian males, this ceremony marked their last direct participation in the church until they decided to marry. However, women continued to attend mass on a fairly regular basis long after they made their confirmation. This boy made his confirmation in Philadelphia in the 1930s.

203. Renewing marriage vows. For their fiftieth anniversary in 1947 Cecilia Rotella Colacino and Savario Colacino renewed their marriage vows in a ceremony conducted in their Brooklyn, New York, home by the parish priest.

204. Death marked a solemn occasion
for the church as well as the family. In
the early twentieth century, wakes took
place in the home amid the cries of
grief-stricken friends and relatives.
Before burial the coffin was carried to
the church and sometimes a band
marched along. This funeral procession
walks toward the first Catholic church
in Helper, Utah.

205. Death cards. People attending
funerals received death cards or buttons
with a picture of the deceased. These
cards were issued in commemoration of
the date of death and included a prayer
for the deceased. Mrs. Concetta Frediani
lived in Toronto, Canada.

L'abbiamo amata durante la sua vita;
lasciate che non l'abbandoniama finche'
non l'abbiamo condotta con le nostre
preghiere nella dimora del Signore:
SANT'AMBROGIO.

IN AMATA MEMORIA

DELLA

Mrs. Concetta Frediani

Beati siano gli afflitti, poiche' saranno
confortati. San Matteo V. 5.

Jesu' mio abbi pieta' sull'anima della

Mrs. Concetta Frediani
Died April 21, 1934
Age 65 years

PREGHIERA

O gentilissimo cuore di Jesu', sempre
presente nell Sac amento dell' Eu-
caristia, sempre consumato con L'amore
ardente per le povere anime del Purga-
torio abbi pieta' sull'anima del tua
scomparsa serva.

Concetta

Non sii severo nel Tuo giudizio ma
lasci che qualche goccia del Tuo Sangue
Prezioso cadi sulle fiamme divoranti e
permetti O Tu Salvatore misericordioso
che i Tuoi Angeli la conducino ad un
luogo di rinfresco, di luce e di pace,
Amen.

Che le Anime di tutti i fedeli scom-
parsi per la misericordia di Dio, riposino
in pace, Amen.

Riposo eterno le sia concesso, O Dio!
e lasci che la luce eterna rivolga su Lei.
Sacro cuore di Jesu' abbi pieta' di Lei.
Cuore Immacolato di Maria, pregate per
Lei. San Giuseppe, amico del Sacro
Cuore pregate per Lei.

(100 giorni per ogni aspirazione)

206. An Italian funeral at Lady of Mount Carmel Church, in Pueblo, Colorado, in 1928. The congregation included Hispanics as well as Italians.

207. Protestant America. Some Italian immigrants felt isolated in Protestant America. If they lived in areas distant from Catholic churches or where American (usually Irish or German) Catholics prevailed, they found little comfort in the restrained services. Protestant missionaries concentrated on providing social services as well as religious training, and some immigrants responded by joining Protestant churches. In Wind Gap, Pennsylvania, Italian immigrants built and then worshiped at St. Mary's Episcopal Church in 1913.

208. Italian Presbyterians. Children of the Esperti, Napolitano, Marino, and LaFata families, who belonged to the First Italian Presbyterian Church in Detroit, enjoy a picnic at Belle Isle, Michigan, in 1910. In immigrant communities the missions provided services to all residents. Children often enjoyed learning crafts, music, and sports at Protestant centers without any loss of commitment to their Catholic faith.

209. Church choir. Sara Russo D'Angelo (seated at the organ) directed and accompanied the first choir at St. Joseph's Roman Catholic Church in Oswego, New York, in 1915. Here Reverend Filomeno Geremia poses with his Italian-American parishioners.

210. St. Gabriel Society. The immigrants brought their devotions to favorite or patron saints to America. In Baltimore, Maryland, Italians established the St. Gabriel Society to worship this saint who had lived in the Abruzzi. In 1928 each of the founders received this certificate of membership. They organized a festival every year that highlighted the parish church's calendar. This certificate belongs to one of the founding members, Tomaso D'Alesandro, who became a U.S. congressman and then the first Italian mayor of Baltimore.

211. Church Scout troop. Italian parishes adopted American organizations that appealed to second-generation Italian Americans. A Boy Scout troop sponsored by the church provided wholesome American activities while protecting youngsters from the proselytizing influence of Protestant or nondenominational Scout troops. Troop 87 met in the basement of the Holy Redeemer Church in St. Paul, Minnesota, in 1928.

212. Altar boys and ushers from Chicago's Our Lady of Pompeii Church traveled to a picnic on this dilapidated, but gaily decorated truck in the 1920s.

170

Congregazione Del S. Cuore Di Gesu. July 16 1936

213. The Congregazione Del Santo Cuore Di Gesu, in Pueblo, Colorado. Seated from left to right are: Bernardina Battaglia, secretary; Domenica Rossorelli, president; Father Salvatore Giglio, Jesuit pastor of Lady of Mount Carmel Church; Angelina Porfilio, vice-president; and Vincenza Riggio, treasurer.

214. The Holy Name Society. An outing of the Holy Name Society of St. Donato's Church in New Haven, Connecticut, in 1936. Three men on the left are holding bocce balls while one member, standing in the third row (right), makes the sign of *mal'occhio*, or the "evil eye," above the heads of two members seated in the second row.

215. The San Antonio di Padua Society, in St. Paul, Minnesota. Members pose with their banner in front of Holy Redeemer Church on June 16, 1940.

216. High school in Ontario. Cardinal Sincero officiates at the opening of Central Boys High School on Main Street, in Hamilton, Ontario, around 1920. In some areas American Catholicism became synonymous with foreignness, and concern over unrestricted immigration often masked a fear of papal interference in a Protestant society.

217. High school in Minnesota. For second-generation Italian Americans church membership could outweigh ethnic identification as common worship in multiethnic parishes stressed the universality of Catholicism. Intermarriage united Italian Americans with other Catholic ethnic groups. School attendance provided one setting for social interaction. This class of 1936 graduated from St. Mary's School in St. Paul, Minnesota.

218. May procession. The national parish church offered the immigrants more than just Italian-speaking priests. Church interiors included the styles, designs, frescoes, favorite saints' statues, and devotional candles that were reminiscent of chapels in Italy. The parish also sponsored activities that combined the Old World devotion with the styles of the New World. Each year, on the first Sunday in May, St. Leo's School in Baltimore, Maryland, held a procession to honor the Blessed Mother. The school band, first communicants, students from each grade, the mothers' club, and sodality marched through the streets of Baltimore's Little Italy. Young girls who had distinguished themselves in school were chosen from the eighth-grade class to carry the statue in the procession. This one dates from around 1938.

219. Pontificio College. Father Domenic Pioletti (seated in the first row, fourth from left) was ordained in 1924 at the Pontificio Collegio dei Sacerdoti per la Emigrazione Italiana in Rome, Italy. Italian priests were trained to care for conationals who emigrated to South and North America. Father Pioletti traveled first to Hibbing, Minnesota, to serve the Italians who worked in the iron mines of that region. He later settled in St. Paul, where he established an Italian national parish at Holy Redeemer Church so that the immigrants would no longer have to worship in what he called "the catacombs" (the basement of the cathedral).

220. Mother Cabrini. Mother Frances Cabrini, the first American saint, founded the Congregation of the Missionary Sisters of the Sacred Heart, which was dedicated to the spiritual care of Italian immigrants. At the turn of the century, Mother Cabrini established hospitals and schools in New Orleans, Chicago, and New York. Shown here is the Mother Cabrini Memorial Hospital in New York City, which was constructed by contributions from her grateful followers and was designed by Anthony De Pace.

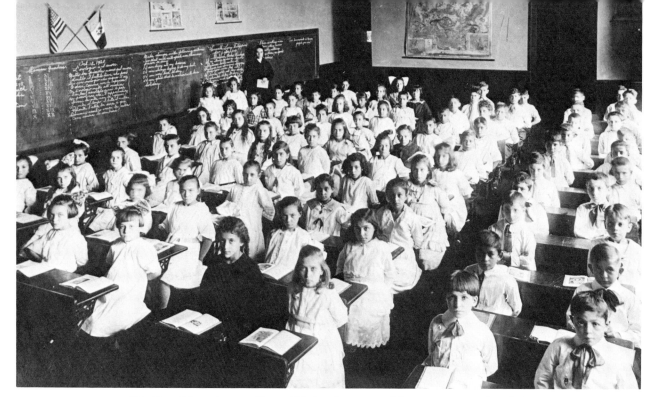

221. Teaching sisters. Sister Ninina Jonata and her grammar-school class at St. Joachim's Church in Trenton, New Jersey, around 1920. The Filippini, a female religious teaching order, founded in Tarquinia, Italy, staffed some of the parochial schools in the Italian national parishes of New Jersey and Maryland. Another teaching order, the Venerini Sisters, founded in Viterbo, Italy, settled in Lawrence and Worcester, Massachusetts, and Providence, Rhode Island.

222. Religious *feste* celebrated in America established an important cultural link for the Italians. The occasion of a saint's day brought together the lay community who helped to organize the events. Religious societies, mutual-benefit societies, church organizations and individuals, and some penitents walking barefoot, all followed the procession through the streets. This view, taken of the Feast of Our Lady of Mount Carmel in Baltimore, Maryland, on July 16, 1922, illustrates the rich pageantry that characterized the immigrants' religious expression.

223. Feast of Santa Rosalia. Sicilian immigrants celebrated the feast of Santa Rosalia (patron saint of Palermo) in their community of Wood River, Illinois, in the 1920s. Many of them had first emigrated to Napoleonville, Louisiana, to work on the sugar-cane plantations. The celebrants carry Italian and American flags to display their respect for the country of their birth and their adopted homeland. In the background, the float from the Italian Lodge of Wood River joins the procession.

224. Neighborhood shrine. Rosaria Catanese (left) stands with her brother, Joe Amato, next to a neighborhood shrine decorated for a feast in Portland, Oregon, in 1910. Rosaria's mother, Natala Amato (right), her sons August and Pete, and her nephews August and Pete Cacicia complete this family's religious commemoration.

225. St. Anthony festival. Special devotion to individual saints took on a new meaning in America. Residents of Baltimore's Little Italy believed that it was St. Anthony of Padua who protected their homes from the disastrous fire of 1904. To commemorate this miracle, they formed a society to celebrate St. Anthony's feast day on June 13. The feast lasted over a week and bands would travel from Philadelphia to play during the celebration. Here the committee poses for its twenty-fifth anniversary.

Photo by F. J. Schaenn

DAL 1904   AL 1929
25.mo Anniversario Della Festa
DI S. ANTONIO DI PADOVA
Comitato Festa Sociale E Coloniale

A. IANNARELLI, PROMOTORE
G. PETRELLA, PRESIDENTE
V. DEL PIZZO, VICE PRESIDENTE
G. B. DURAZZO, SEGRETARIO
GIOVANNI, COSSENTINO VICE SEGRETARIO
G. FULLANO, TESORIERE
P. MAROCCO, COMITATO COL. E. PRES. SOCIALE
V. SUGAMOSTO, GRAN MARESCIALLO
           P. SILVESTRI, CURATORE

A TIROCCHI, MARESCIALLO
GIUSEPPE, COSSENTINO, MARESCIALLO
A. SCISCIONE COMITATO BENEMERITO
PAOLO CASTELLO, CURATORE
F. SOPINO, COMIT. D'ONORE ALLA PROCESSIONE
A. TARADDEO,
F. PETRELLI, COMIT
VINCENZO BEALE

226. Italian parade. Italian members of a mutual aid society of Holy Ghost Church in Providence, Rhode Island, march down Atwells Avenue in 1906.

227. St. Joseph's Day at home. The Old World tradition of the St. Joseph's Day celebration continued in America with food of banquet proportions covering the table, which was placed in front of a shrine to the Holy Family. Children dressed as St. Joseph and Mary, the Blessed Mother, and others dressed as angels visited each home and "blessed" the food, which was then shared by relatives, friends, and neighbors. This celebration took place in Hamilton, Ontario, in 1941.

6
ETHNIC ORGANIZATIONS

228. The Società Italiana di Mutua Beneficenza Maria Immacolata Concezione.
Members of this society gather in White Castle, Louisiana, to celebrate the feast
day of the Blessed Virgin on December 8, 1919. The society was formed in 1904
by men who had emigrated from towns in central Sicily. Members contributed
toward an illness and death benefit fund to aid their families. In the event of a
death, members of the society attended the funeral. Each year on December 8,
the society formed a procession to the church, where a *messa cantata,* including
a sermon in Italian, was offered. A band played for the parade and the services.
In the evening a dance was held for the entire community and out-of-town
guests. Proceeds from the dance went to worthy causes. For example, in 1917
the proceeds went toward the relief of Italian families suffering from the effects
of World War I.

The immigrant's need to join with others of common background or interest fostered the formation of associations for Italian Americans. *Paese* or regional origins served as a basis for establishing many groups. The Calaseibetta Society of Baltimore admitted men who were born in that central Sicilian town. In San Francisco the Luccese del Mondo followed similar criteria. All these groups sponsored formal and informal social activities, ranging from annual dinners or picnics to card playing at club headquarters. Most also offered mutual-benefit services. Members paid dues that gave them illness and death insurance. A sick member could go to the doctor retained by the association. He was entitled to a sum of money to help his family when he could not work. Upon his death, his widow received a sum from the association. Social obligations accompanied the benefits. A delegation visited the sick and the entire association attended the funeral of any member. Such organizations existed in Italy but they had greater significance in America, where the immigrant was distant from the extended family networks that offered social and economic aid in times of emergency.

Some organizations were formed on the basis of occupation or class, such as the Fratellanza Minatori, whose members were miners, or the Società Operaia di M.S. San Francisco, whose members were all types of workers. Most groups participated in their communities' celebrations commemorating Columbus Day. Those associations devoted to a patron saint arranged special activities for the saint's day—usually a procession and a mass.

Italian immigrants also founded organizations to meet the new conditions of their lives. Political clubs affiliated with one of the major parties promoted the official nominees and encouraged immigrants to become citizens. At first, political associations supported the party candidate, who was usually a non-Italian. In most areas, Italians did not have a sufficient number of registered voters to determine elections, but by the turn of the century, both parties appealed to the Italian-American voter, either by appointing a conational to a status position in the party or in government or by endorsing a conational for elected office. By the 1930s Italian-American votes could influence the outcome of elections in some cities. Finally, Italian-American political organizations promoted candidates from their own community. Angelo Rossi of San Francisco and Robert Maestri of New Orleans became mayors; Thomas D'Alesandro of Baltimore and Vito Marcantonio of New York became United States congressmen.

The Order Sons of Italy in America, established in 1905, represented another type of response to the New World. This organization promoted a love of the motherland and loyalty toward the adopted countries of North America. The Order attempted to dispel the anti-Italian prejudice that associated immigrants and their descendants with the crime and vice that plagued American cities. Lodges formed across North America, supporting worthy causes in Italy—such as the Italian War Relief of 1918—and in America—such as orphanages. Pride in the Italian heritage grew in proportion to the anti-immigrant policies of the 1920s and 1930s. And organizations like the Order Sons of Italy saw themselves as the sole support of immigrant self-respect.

The 1920s and 1930s were years of transition. Children (the second generation) of the immigrants began to participate more fully in the social and economic life of America. Their achievement was recognized in the formation of professional organizations, such as the Italian American Graduate Club of New Orleans, which admitted persons who acquired a bachelor's degree, and the Justinian Society of Chicago for Italian-American lawyers. Both the organizations carried over from Italy, and the new ones formed in America promoted ethnic consciousness. The accomplishment of individuals became a source of pride for the Italian-American community.

SOCIETA' SVIZZERE.

HELVETIA

SOCIETA' SVIZZERA DI MUTUA BENEFICENZA
SAN FRANCISCO.

Questa societá che è stata riorganizzata nel 1874 ha ora un
capitale che supera la somma di venti mila dollari con un
numero di menbri di 400 circa.

La società conta molti soci degenti alla compagna; anzi
nei centri popolosi come Petaluma, San José, Santa Cruz,
Stockton, Sacramento St. Helena, Napa, Volcano, Mok.
Hill, Nevada City, Sonoma, vi è un agente incaricato di cor-
rispondere colla Direzione in San Francisco.

Di 84 società svizzere di beneficenza esistenti all'estero
quella di San Francisco può andar orgogliosa per l'elevatezza

229. Società Svizzere. Immigrants from northern Italy settled in the San Francisco area in the mid-nineteenth century. Some from the Italian-speaking cantons of Switzerland formed their own organization in 1874. Most of the mutual-benefit organizations reflected the geographic origins of its members.

230. The Matrice Club of Cleveland, Ohio, was established in 1918 by immigrants from the town of Matrice in the Abruzzi. For many Italians membership in associations helped them to reunite with *paesani*.

231. Società Operaia Italiana di Mutuo Soccorso. Members attend a banquet on May 19, 1912, at the Fior D'Italia Restaurant in San Francisco. Notice the two bottles of wine (one white, one red) in front of each place setting. This organization admitted laborers who combined the advantage of illness and death benefits with opportunities for socializing.

232. Unione Italiana at Seventh Avenue and Eighteenth Street in Ybor City, Tampa, Florida, was organized as a mutual aid society in 1894. The first president, Bartolio Filogamo, was also the first Italian cigar manufacturer (the Alvarez Cigar Factory) in Tampa. The Unione offered its members a comprehensive health-insurance program, distinguishing it as one of the oldest cooperative medical plans in the United States.

233. The Loggia Cristoforo Colombo was established by Italian copper miners in Jerome, Arizona, in 1931. In this picture the members wear their lodge badges. Usually the reverse side of the badge was black, allowing it to be used by the official delegation to attend a member's funeral.

234. The Società di Mutuo Soccorso I Voluntari Cilentani honored the volunteers from the region of Cilento in the province of Salerno who fought with Giuseppi Garibaldi. Immigrants from Cilento who settled in Paterson, New Jersey, founded the organization in 1889. In this 1938 picture, members are gathered at an outing in Hawthorne, New Jersey.

188

235. Italian band. Many Italians played musical instruments. In America they formed bands to play on festive occasions, such as Columbus Day. This Italian band entertained the community of Morenci, Arizona.

236. Order of Odd Fellows. When Italians formed the exclusively Italian Dante Lodge, they adopted the American International Order of Odd Fellows as a fraternal organization in Alderson, Oklahoma, in 1915. This demonstrated their ability to use an American organization to retain their ethnic identity.

237. Scavenger's Protection Association. Members of this association, founded by immigrants from Genoa, escort the body of a member in his funeral procession on Columbus Avenue in North Beach, San Francisco, in 1910.

238. The Fratellanza Minatori attend the funeral of a member at the cemetery in Sunnyside, Utah, in 1920.

Order Sons of Italy in America

WHAT IS IT?

The ORDER is a voluntary fraternal organization on the lodge system, with a representative form of government.

The ORDER believes that all men were created equal; that all Christian creeds should be given due respect, as well as political opinions. It believes in the promotion of the moral, intellectual and material improvement of its members, and of all humanity. It believes in waging war against prejudice and superstition. It believes in spreading the conviction that it is the duty of every man or woman to take part in all activities of the Canadian life and thus make this activity a factor for social and moral improvement.

LIBERTY—EQUALITY—FRATERNITY is the motto of our organization:

LIBERTY—We wish freedom of thought, creeds, politics and teaching. We desire that true freedom which alone can bring all men and women to the same higher spiritual, moral and intellectual plane, that freedom which spreads over people the salutary enlightenment of knowledge in order to make of them a thinking and acting conscious body.

EQUALITY—We want to do away with privileges and all sorts of slavery and give equal rights to all, as well as a generous effusion of the gifts of nature and the fruits of the land, so that every man may bless the soil and fellowship of men.

FRATERNITY—We are eager to stretch forth our loving hand to the lowly and good without any distinction whatever. We are eager to care for the child, who will be the man or the woman of tomorrow; to aid the poor and provide shelter for the homeless. We want to protect woman, the mother of humanity of the future, and to alleviate the distress of those that suffer, of the widows and unfortunate babies. Wherever there is an unhappy and sorrowing fellow man we will stretch out a helping hand; wherever a human being suffers intellectual or economical hardship there we will bring words of love and comfort, and accomplish deeds that will touch, alleviate and uplift. We want every man, woman or child to have a square deal and fair play.

The ORDER wishes to cultivate mutual benevolence and human consideration; it wishes to cultivate and improve the minds of all with those ideals which are in accord with the modern conception of true and social democracy. It desires to show that the Italians possess such mental and moral qualities as to make them not only precious workingmen but also an efficient factor for human progress and social greatness. It aims principally to do all that can be done to make good Canadian citizens out of the people of Italian origin residing in this country, and, by cultivating in them the peculiar good qualities of the race, fit them so that they may successfully contribute and give of their best to the upbuilding of Canada, which is in the mind and in the heart of all those who truly love this country and work with deep interest for its development.

The ORDER feels that the true greatness of a nation is not made up only of dollars, goods and other forms of material wealth which it may possess, but that it is also made of the traditions, the history, the literature, the arts, the love for the country and the spiritual unfaltering devotion to duty of the whole people.

This is summarily the program of the ORDER SONS OF ITALY IN AMERICA.

239. The Order Sons of Italy in America was established in 1905. Soon chapters formed across North America. This description of the organization served the Italian lodges in Canada. The order's purpose was to maintain a respect for its Italian heritage while participating as a full member of its adopted nation.

240. La Nuova Sicilia Lodge, Order Sons of Italy in America, held this picnic in 1924 in Ybor City, Tampa, Florida. Most Italians in Tampa emigrated from Sicily. Proceeds from this picnic were donated to the Tampa Children's Home.

241. Oswego Sons of Italy. A 1906 lodge of the Sons of Italy posing in Oswego, New York, later became known as the Dante Alighieri Lodge.

242. Young Men's Lincoln Club. Naturalization or participation in the American political system was one sign of assimilation for the immigrant. While the Democratic party had traditionally welcomed new Americans to its ranks, at the turn of the century the Republicans also began to recruit immigrants. In some sections of America, the Irish-dominated Democratic machine was not eager to open its ranks and share power with the Italians. Here the Young Men's Lincoln Club of Little Italy in New York City celebrate Lincoln's birthday in 1915.

243. Candidate. Vincent Palmisano, an immigrant from Termini Imerese, Sicily, ran for Baltimore City Council in 1915. His conationals in the Third Ward Democratic Club formed a power base for his career. He was elected to the House of Representatives in 1926—the first person of Italian birth to sit in that legislative body.

244. Antony Di Marco. A coalition of Italian-American organizations supported the efforts of Maryland State Assemblyman Antony Di Marco in 1909 to sponsor a bill declaring Columbus Day a legal holiday in that state. Maryland was the second state in the Union (Colorado was the first) to commemorate formally this significant American event.

The Justinian Society of Lawyers of Chicago Circa 1931

FEDERAZIONE

Opposite:
245. Justinian Society of Lawyers.
Italian college graduates, professionals, and successful businessmen formed organizations that recognized their accomplishments in American society. The Justinian Society of Lawyers was founded in Chicago around 1931. There is also a Justinian Society of Jurists that enrolls U.S. judges of Italian-American heritage.

246. Federazione Columbiana. Most Italian organizations, especially those named after a famous explorer, such as the Federazione Columbiana Lodge No. 68 of Bingham County, Utah, participated in Columbus Day celebrations. Many communities sponsored a parade and held a ceremony with speeches given by American political officials and leaders of the Italian-American community.

247. The Unione Italiana of New Orleans collected food each year to make Christmas baskets for the less fortunate members of the Italian community. This picture, taken around 1935, illustrates how most ethnic groups helped care for their own. Until the New Deal relief programs, these projects often constituted the only source of aid to families of the unemployed.

7
ETHNIC PERSISTENCE

248. Women and politics. Italian-American political activity expanded as the second generation grew to maturity. Early in the twentieth century, most associations and the Italian-language press urged the immigrants to become American citizens. Both major parties recruited members from this potentially powerful voting bloc. Women, too, played an increasingly important role in party functions. Here the Women's Auxiliary Convention Committee of the Columbian Republican party meets in 1946 to support Thomas E. Dewey as governor for New York State.

What is an Italian American? Who are they? Since World War II, the majority of people in the United States who claim Italian heritage are third generation. Many have memories of grandparents who spoke little or no English, yet they see little in their daily lives that connects with those memories. The Canadian experience differs because of that nation's immigration policy, which enabled thousands to enter in the 1950s. Canadian Italians, therefore, have a new immigrant generation that assumed leadership roles in preserving the Italian language and culture. Even so, as the generational distance between first arrival and contemporary assimilated life-styles increases, shall the immigrant culture disappear?

The heritage of a people can continue in a variety of ways. There are the obvious visual elements of customs, dress, life choices (endogamy), and retention of language; the less obvious ones are culture, attitudes and beliefs, and preferences in life-styles.

Since most people do not analyze why they do things or think about things in certain ways, it is difficult for the majority of Italians to pinpoint any continuity in heritage. It is also difficult for the scholar—the social scientist who observes and measures behavior. Are Italian-American family attitudes different in degree from those of Polish Americans? Is the fact that more Italian Americans are in blue-collar occupations, rather than in the professions, a statement of lack of upward mobility, prejudice, and discrimination, or perhaps a preference for the craft traditions that the third generation inherited from their fathers and grandfathers? The issue of the meaning of Italian-American identity and the persistence of their ethnicity is fraught with the dangers of overgeneralization, vagueness in interpretation and definition of terms.

In postwar America, Italian Americans shared in the hopes and dreams for a peaceful world in which their children would prosper. They felt a special *simpatico* for the problems of Italy. Committees set up relief funds to aid those in Italy who suffered from the devastation of war. Italians contributed as individuals and as groups. They also influenced the activities of American organizations, such as the International Ladies Garment Workers Union, which established a trade school at Montebello outside Palermo. Natural disasters, such as floods and earthquakes, bring the Italian-American community forward to offer help. Across North America great efforts were made to aid those who suffered in the 1980 earthquakes in southern Italy.

A review of Italian-American involvement in and contribution to North America reads like a cavalcade of stars. The children and grandchildren of immigrants have achieved success in many areas, ranging from politics to the arts. Whether achievement in certain fields, such as the arts and drama, reflects a cultural preference on the part of Italian Americans is again a difficult issue. Rosa Ponselle and Gian-Carlo Menotti may have been more inclined to follow their careers in opera and music because this tradition is a favored one for Italians. In other areas such as sports, some say that the combination of street-wise gamesmanship and the attraction of professional careers intertwine so that talented Italian-American boxers, football players, and baseball players move from their boyhood games into the major leagues.

Although each ethnic group is proud of those who achieve the acclaim of the larger society, continuity of ethnicity is measured more by the daily lives of Italian Americans. As the population scatters and intermarries, what happens to the Italian-American identity? Some traditions disappear, others continue in an altered fashion. No longer do the immigrants from the Sicilian provinces of Messina and Catania gather on 13th Street between Avenue A and 1st Avenue in Manhattan to celebrate the feast of the Black Saint (the Madonna of Tindari), but it seems that half of the population of metropolitan New York attends the enlarged and extended San Gennaro feast each September in Little Italy. Population moves often result in the regrouping of Italians. In the Sunbelt areas new lodges of the Sons of Italy form. In the 1980s a move to Fort Lauderdale, Florida, or Scottsdale, Arizona, need not signal the end to family dinners of lasagne and ravioli and tasty Italian bread. Ethnic family businesses follow the population trends. In a limited way the internal migration follows some of the patterns of the transatlantic crossing. In the older neighborhoods, ethnic federation occurs as the Italian community expands to include the newer immigrants. Therefore, an Italian bakery sells Portuguese bread, and an Italian parish includes the newer Chinese communicants in its Columbus Day celebrations.

Rites of passage still retain elements of the Italian heritage. The third generation badgers the second generation for recipes of traditional holiday dishes. The choice of godparents still implies a special relation and obligation. Intermarriage often means a dualism (both traditions coexisting), rather than a fusion or loss of tradition.

American society seems to guarantee some ethnic continuity. As "foreign" ways become part of a more sophisticated, tolerant, and curious native population, each ethnic group finds encouragement in the interest taken in its festivals, cuisine, and language. With this endorsement of things Italian and Italian American, the children of the immigrants can choose to declare themselves the special beneficiaries of the simple as well as the grand legacy that belongs to all Americans.

249. Fiorello La Guardia entered public life in the first decade of the twentieth century. As a lawyer, he helped striking garment workers, many of whom were Italian and Jewish. He served in the U.S. Congress, and in 1933 became mayor of New York City. Here he meets with former Vice-President Henry Wallace.

250. The mayoralty of New York. In 1949 Vito Marcantonio, former U.S. congressman, ran unsuccessfully against William O'Dwyer in the race for mayor of New York City. However, O'Dwyer resigned the following year to accept the post as ambassador to Mexico, and in the special election to replace him, three Italian Americans were pitted against each other: Republican Edward Corsi, Democrat Ferdinand Pecora, and Experience party candidate Vincent Impellitieri, who was the victor. This recognition of the importance of the role of Italian Americans in commanding the endorsement of members within their group as well as outside seemed to promise success similar to that of the Irish Americans. Yet as Italian Americans gained their opportunity, campaigns based on broad reform issues representing broad-based support replaced the traditional party-dominated elections.

251. Italian-American judge. From the New Deal to the present, the participation of Italian Americans in public office has increased. Both as elected and appointed officials, Italian Americans serve at every level of public administration across North America. Here New York City's Mayor Robert Wagner administers the oath of office to Louis Paganico as justice of the Court of Domestic Relations in 1955.

252. Italian-American senator. John Pastore of Rhode Island, elected to the U.S. Senate in 1950, was the first Italian American to serve in that body.

253. Italian-American congressman.
Peter Rodino, U.S. congressman from Newark, New Jersey, expresses his concern for foreign-born Americans by monitoring immigration legislation. His role as chairman of the House Investigating Committee during the Watergate crisis earned him praise from both the international as well as the national community. Here Rodino and Essex County clerk Nick Caputo campaign with Democratic party nominee George McGovern. In 1967 Rodino was the recipient of the Guglielmo Marconi Award, presented to him by the Order Sons of Italy.

254. Mario Lanza and Jimmy Durante.
Perhaps the role of Italian Americans in the arts and the performing arts has received the highest acclaim from the public. In the early nineteenth century, Italian musicians played in the U.S. armed services bands; opera singers, such as Adelina Patti, toured American cities; Constantino Brumidi's frescoes decorated the Capitol; and Luigi Palma di Cesnola was director of the Metropolitan Museum of Art. This contribution continued in the twentieth century with the spectacular careers of Enrico Caruso and Rudolph Valentino. Here comedian Jimmy Durante compares vocal chords with singer Mario Lanza.

255. Comedian Pat Cooper (born Pasquale Caputo) uses his own ethnic experience as a source for humor. One of his famous lines is a question heard in most Italian-American kitchens on Sunday afternoon, "Is the water boiling?" (Since Sunday has traditionally been a day of family gathering, Italian Americans continue to follow custom by serving pasta.)

256. Dean Martin, Frank Sinatra, and **Judy Garland.** The careers of all three include recording, television, and films. Sinatra symbolizes for many Italian Americans the success story with flair— from Hoboken to Hollywood.

257. Caterina Valente is one of the many Italian-American entertainers who are active in the recording industry.

258. The Coppola family. Francis Ford Coppola, his father, Carmine, and his sister, Talia Shire, admire the Oscars won for the film they created, *The Godfather.* Carmine Coppola wrote the musical score, Francis directed, and Talia played one of the Corleone family.

259. Ben Gazzara, born in New York City to Antonio and Angelina (Cusumano) Gazzara, began his acting career in the 1950s. He has been featured in such films as *Anatomy of a Murder* (1959), *The Young Doctors* (1961), and *Al Capone* (1974). Some of his stage appearances include *Cat on a Hot Tin Roof* (1955) and *End As A Man* (1953), for which he won the Drama Critics Award.

260. Liza Minelli, daughter of producer/director Vincente Minelli and singer Judy Garland has developed a career in film, theater, and music.

206

261. Richard Castellano (right), who played the father in *Lovers and Other Strangers*, enjoys lunch at Nicastro's in Newark, New Jersey. Castellano was nominated for an Academy Award in 1972 for his role in *The Godfather*.

262. Sylvester Stallone wrote, directed, and starred in his films *Rocky I*, *Rocky II*, and *Rocky III*. Here he plays a union organizer in the movie *F.I.S.T.*

263. Rosa Ponselle. When Rosa Ponselle made her debut as Leonora at the
Metropolitan Opera on November 15, 1918, she sang opposite the famous tenor
Enrico Caruso. In the finale of *La Forza del Destino*, Ponselle, Caruso as Don
Alvaro, and José Mardones as Fra Melitone joined in a memorable trio.

265. Edward Villella established a brilliant career as one of the leading dancers of the New York City Ballet. Villella has gone on to teach ballet and write and produce television productions.

264. Gian-Carlo Menotti was born in Cadegliano, Italy, and came to America in 1928. His music, especially his operas, is well known to North Americans. His *Amahl and the Night Visitors* is performed or played during Christmas. *The Saint of Bleecker Street* vividly portrays the lives of Italians in Greenwich Village. Menotti was a recipient of the Guggenheim Award in 1946 and 1947, and he was awarded the Pulitzer Prize for music in 1950 and 1954.

266. Albert Innaurato, from South Philadelphia, uses his Italian-American experiences in his work. His comedy *Gemini*, which enjoyed a long run on Broadway, focuses on the trials and tribulations of an Italian-American family living in working-class row houses in Philadelphia and how they react to a weekend visit from upper-class New Englanders.

267. The Yankee Clipper. Joe Di Maggio is cheered by the fans at Yankee Stadium on a day commemorating him in October 1949. Mel Allen is the master of ceremonies. The long list of successful Italian Americans in baseball includes Yogi Berra, catcher for the Yankees; Phil Cavaretta, first baseman for the Chicago Cubs; Sal Maglie, pitcher for the New York Giants; Ralph Branca, pitcher for the New York Dodgers; Carl Furillo, Dodger outfielder; Joe Garagiola, catcher for the Pirates and Cardinals; and Phil Rizzuto, Yankee shortstop. Both Joe Garagiola and Phil Rizzuto continue their careers as sports announcers.

268. Andy Robustelli played defensive end for the New York Giants football team from 1956 to 1964, and later managed the team. His teammates valued his aggressive and skillful playing style and chose him as their defensive captain. He was elected to the Football Hall of Fame.

269. Phil Esposito, known as "Mr. Clutch," played a strong center for the New York Rangers. A Canadian Italian, Esposito first joined the Chicago Black Hawks in 1963. In 1967 he played for the Boston Bruins, helping them win the Stanley Cup Championship.

271. Giorgio Chinaglia plays forward on the Cosmos soccer team. The growing popularity of soccer in North America indicates the continuing influence of the Old World upon the New World. Chinaglia developed his playing skill in Italy.

270. Mario Andretti, born in Montona, Trieste, Italy, came to America in 1955 and was naturalized an American citizen in 1959. His international reputation as a race-car driver grew out of his successful bids for the Grand Prix and other racing events. Because of the obvious danger of this sport, many of Andretti's safety innovations have been adopted by some of the leading automobile manufacturers.

272. Rocky Casale, an Italian-American boxer, is one of the many Italian-American boxers who have held championship titles. Other champions are Rocky Marciano, heavyweight champion from Brockton, Massachusetts; Rocky Graziano, middleweight champion from New York City; and Tony Canzoneri and Lou Ambers (D'Ambriosio), lightweight champions from New York.

273. Anthony Abbatiello—jockey.

274. Edward Pellegrino serves as president of Catholic University. Some of the Jesuit universities such as Georgetown and San Francisco had Italians as their first presidents.

275. Feast of the Assumption. Italian musicians in Boston's municipal band are pleased with the contributions they helped collect during the procession for the Feast of the Assumption.

276. One hundredth anniversary. Parishioners of St. Mary Magdalen di Pazzi Church of Philadelphia mark the one hundredth anniversary of this Italian national parish in 1958.

Opposite:
277. San Gennaro Festival. The celebration for San Gennaro, patron saint of Naples, served to unite Neapolitan immigrants in America. Here in New York's Little Italy, the saint's shrine lights the sky. This feast has become an attraction for all New Yorkers. Thousands of people stroll past the stalls, savoring the smell of zeppole, sausages, calzone, and pizza.

278. Sicilian cacti. Tony Diecidue, a retired produce dealer in Tampa, Florida, poses in front of his Ficco di India (prickly pear) plants. These cacti grow in Sicily and are cultivated for their fruit in Florida, Arizona, and California.

279. Canadian Italians. Railroad workers from Treviso and Friuli-Venezia, spend their Sunday off in Picton, Ontario, in 1954, performing a spoof wedding. The Canadian postwar immigration policy attracted thousands of Italians to settle there. Because of this recent migration, their communities reflect an *ambiente* that features their Italian heritage and language. Italian Canadians rally to the cause of bilingualism in public education and follow their own form of ethnic politics.

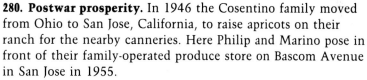

280. Postwar prosperity. In 1946 the Cosentino family moved from Ohio to San Jose, California, to raise apricots on their ranch for the nearby canneries. Here Philip and Marino pose in front of their family-operated produce store on Bascom Avenue in San Jose in 1955.

281. Modernization. Mr. and Mrs. Cosentino surrounded by their sons (left to right) Salvatore, Domenic, Philip, and Marino at the 1971 opening of their large, modern supermarket across the street from their older store in San Jose.

282. An artisan of today. Even in the postindustrial age a few artisans retain their pride and devotion to family tradition. Antonio Gagliarducci, a knife and scissors grinder in St. Louis, still pushes his cart through the streets as he did in 1925, when he emigrated from southern Italy.

283. Barbershop. Pete "Figo" Carvella (left) decorates his New Castle, Pennsylvania, barbershop with photos of famous American sports figures; over 90 percent are Italian American. Cavella's nickname, "Figo," derives from the character Figaro in the opera *The Barber of Seville.* He carries on the business begun by his father in 1922.

284. Sunday dinner. Relatives gathering to enjoy food and companionship remains the central focus for most Italian-American families. Here the Gentile family eat and talk in their Queens, New York, home in 1950.

285. Balducci's Market, on the Avenue of the Americas in Manhattan's
Greenwich Village, offers the entire range of Italian groceries, including
prepared foods and cookies.

286. Quincy Market. Open-air vending at Boston's Quincy Market retains some of the Old World tradition of bringing daily activities out into the streets.

287. An Italian fish store at Park Avenue and 116th Street in New York's East Harlem offers such delicacies as *pulpo,* or baby octopus. *Pulpo* is a dish that is prepared by many Italian-American families during the Christmas holidays.

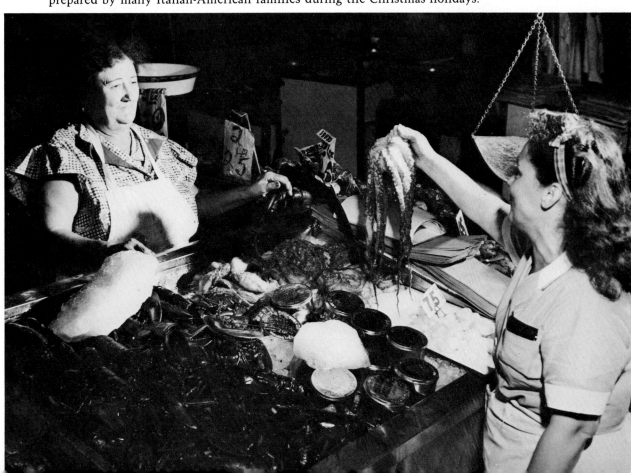

288. Thanksgiving Day celebrated Italian-American style in Brooklyn, New York, 1950. The joining together of two cultures for the Gerardi clan meant traditional American holiday fare coupled with traditional Italian dishes. The menu began with turkey giblet soup, followed by pasta, then meat that was prepared in spaghetti sauce; next, the turkey was served with dressing, yams, cranberry sauce, salad; and the meal was topped off with a sweet course, consisting of homemade pumpkin and apple pies, Italian pastries, nuts, fruits, and coffee. Some form of pasta was necessary to add a festive note to Sunday meals and certainly to important occasions, such as Thanksgiving. (Fourth of July picnics also reflected this combination—a lunch of baked macaroni, veal cutlets, and salad would be followed with a late afternoon "snack" of frankfurters and hamburgers.)

290. Ethnic combination. Contact between ethnic communities resulted in a combination of Italian and Portuguese baked goods in Toronto, Canada. The area, formerly Italian, now includes more recently arrived Portuguese. Businesses originally designed to serve the Italian ethnic community are expanding and attracting the newcomers.

Opposite:

289. Christmas recipes for special fish dishes, cakes, and cookies remain part of most family traditions. Josephine Dalessandro, left, Angelina Pilardi and Antoinette Mascia, right, chat at the kitchen table in 1956 in Pittsburgh, Pennsylvania, after preparing antipasto for the holiday meal. Notice the plates of *dolci* and baked goods.

SS Peter & Paul's Church
Columbus
FESTIVAL
3 BIG DAYS

Friday,   Oct. 10th – 7–10 p.m.
Saturday, Oct. 11th – 1–10 p.m.
Sunday,   Oct. 12th – 1–10 p.m.

Games, Entertainment, Booths!

SATURDAY
1–8 P.M.
CHINESE DINNER

SUNDAY
1–8 P.M.
Italian Dinner

SS Peter & Paul's AUDITORIUM **Powell & Filbert Streets**

291. **Ethnic harmony** assumes different combinations in different locations. San Francisco's North Beach, once a Little Italy, now contains Chinese Americans—an extension of that city's Chinatown. The Salesians at St. Peter and Paul's acknowledge this change by providing Chinese as well as Italian-speaking priests for confessions. In this setting Columbus Day becomes an American festival with both a Chinese and an Italian flair.

292. **Ristorante Puglia,** a *casalingo,* or family-style restaurant, in New York's Little Italy, specializes in the dishes prepared in the southeastern region of Italy more commonly referred to as Bari by Italian Americans.

226

293. Bocce on the beach. Italian Americans play a game of bocce in Monterey, California, where many Italian Americans continue to earn their living in the fishing industry.

PICTURE CREDITS

1. Courtesy of Carlo Ferroni.
2. Carpenter Center for the Visual Arts, Harvard University.
3. Centro Studi Emigrazione, Roma.
4. Courtesy of Attilio Campolongo.
5. From *L'Illustrazione Italiana* (1904).
6. Ibid.
7. Courtesy of Attilio Campolongo.
8. From *L'Illustrazione Italiana* (1891).
9. From *L'Illustrazione Italiana* (1904).
10. Maryland Historical Society.
11. From *L'Illustrazione Italiana* (no year given).
12. Ibid.
13. Ibid.
14. Courtesy of Dante and Rose Fantasia.
15. From *Two Rosetos* by Carla Bianco.
16. Courtesy of Julia Santini.
17. From *L'Illustrazione Italiana* (no year given).
18. Centro Studi Emigrazione, Roma.
19. Multicultural History Society of Ontario.
20. U.S. Information Agency No. 90-6-73-1 in the National Archives.
21. Multicultural History Society of Ontario.
22. Photograph by Jacob A. Riis, Jacob A. Riis Collection, Museum of the City of New York.
23. The Balch Institute.
24. Library of Congress.
25. Lewis W. Hine Collection, Local History and Genealogy Division, New York Public Library, Astor, Lenox and Tilden Foundations.
26. Library of Congress, Bain Collection.
27. The New York Public Library, Astor, Lenox and Tilden Foundations.
28. Carpenter Center for the Visual Arts, Harvard University.
29. From *L'Illustrazione Italiana* (1902).
30. Lewis W. Hine Collection, Local History and Genealogy Division, New York Public Library, Astor, Lenox and Tilden Foundations.
31. New York Public Library.
32. Library of Congress.
33. From *Almanaco Italo Svizzero Americana* (1881); The Balch Institute.

34. From *Columbus Revista* magazine (1925).
35. From *Almanaco Italo Svizzero Americana* (1881); The Balch Institute.
36. Photograph by Jacob A. Riis, Jacob A. Riis Collection, Museum of the City of New York.
37. Photograph by Lewis Hine, from *America and Lewis Hine*; collection of Walter and Naomi Rosenblum.
38. Nebraska State Historical Society.
39. Carpenter Center for the Visual Arts, Harvard University.
40. Minnesota Historical Society.
41. Arizona Historical Foundation, Hayden Library, Arizona State University.
42. Eureka Federal Savings North Beach Museum, San Francisco.
43. University of Texas Institute of Texan Cultures.
44. J. Ulmer Collection, University of Alaska Archives, Fairbanks.
45. Multicultural History Society of Ontario.
46. Western History Collections, University of Oklahoma Library.
47. U.S. Information Agency No. 208-FS-941-1 in the National Archives.
48. Courtesy of Frank and Sarah (Ferrante) Giordano.
49. Western Research Collection, Pueblo Library District.
50. Lewis W. Hine Collection, Library of Congress.
51. Utah State Historical Society.
52. Courtesy of Julia Santini.
53. Courtesy of Mr. and Mrs. Frank Scarpaci.
54. Courtesy of Julia Santini.
55. Ibid.
56. Lewis W. Hine Collection, Library of Congress.
57. Ibid.
58. Courtesy of Ioli Giomi.
59. Connecticut Historical Society.
60. Courtesy of Julia Santini.
61. Smithsonian Institution.
62. Library of Congress, photo by Frank Delano.
63. Maryland Historical Society.
64. Nebraska State Historical Society.
65. Nevada Historical Society.
66. University of Illinois Library at Chicago Circle Campus, Jane Addams Memorial Collection.
67. Courtesy of Nicholas Sammartino.
68. Courtesy of George Pasadore.
69. Minnesota Historical Society.
70. Multicultural History Society of Ontario.
71. Courtesy of George Pasadore.
72. Texas Pacific Oil Company, from a copy at the University of Texas Institute of Texan Cultures.
73. Photograph by Lewis W. Hine, from *America & Lewis Hine*; collection of Naomi and Walter Rosenblum.
74. Ibid.

75. Western Reserve Historical Society.
76. Maryland Historical Society.
77. New Jersey Historical Society.
78. *Italian Tribune News*, Ace Alagna, publisher.
79. Multicultural Historical Society of Ontario.
80. Courtesy of Nicholas Sammartino.
81. Eureka Federal Savings North Beach Museum, San Francisco.
82. Courtesy of Anthony Pizzo.
83. Courtesy of Nick and Anna Pavia.
84. Western Research Collection, Pueblo Library District.
85. Multicultural History Society of Ontario.
86. Immigration History Research Center, University of Minnesota.
87. Ibid.
88. Both photos from The Balch Institute.
89. Photograph by Jacob A. Riis, Jacob A. Riis Collection, Museum of the City of New York.
90. Eureka Federal Savings North Beach Museum, San Francisco.
91. Courtesy of Anthony Pizzo.
92. Photograph by Jacob A. Riis, Jacob A. Riis Collection, Museum of the City of New York.
93. Western Reserve Historical Society.
94. The City of Toronto Archives.
95. Western Reserve Historical Society.
96. University of Illinois Library at Chicago Circle Campus, Jane Addams Memorial Collection.
97. Lewis W. Hine Collection, Library of Congress.
98. Library of Congress.
99. The City of Toronto Archives.
100. Pennsylvania Historical and Museum Commission.
101. Lewis W. Hine Collection, Library of Congress.
102. International Museum of Photography, George Eastman House, Rochester, New York.
103. Utah State Historical Society.
104. From *Columbus Revista* magazine (1920s).
105. Arizona Historical Foundation, Hayden Library, Arizona State University.
106. West Virginia and Regional History Collection, West Virginia University Library.
107. The City of Toronto Archives.
108. Merrimack Valley Textile Museum.
109. Idaho State Historical Society.
110. Courtesy of Jo Ann Pilardi Fuchs.
111. Courtesy of Carlo Ferroni.
112. U.S. Information Agency No. 208-FS-2159-4 in the National Archives.
113. University of North Carolina Library.
114. Courtesy of Anthony Pizzo.
115. Eureka Federal Savings North Beach Museum, San Francisco.

116. Photo by Marion Post Wolcott for the Farm Security Administration, Library of Congress.
117. U.S. Information Agency No. 208-FS-850-2 in the National Archives.
118. Lewis W. Hine Collection, Library of Congress.
119. Ibid.
120. Ibid.
121. Ibid.
122. Ibid.
123. Ibid.
124. Carpenter Center for the Visual Arts, Harvard University.
125. Lewis W. Hine Collection, Library of Congress.
126. Maryland Historical Society.
127. Courtesy of Joseph Dell'Alba.
128. Lewis W. Hine Collection, Library of Congress.
129. Archives of Labor and Urban Affairs, Wayne State University.
130. Eureka Federal Savings North Beach Museum, San Francisco.
131. Nebraska State Historical Society.
132. Ibid.
133. Courtesy of Luciano Iorizzo.
134. Courtesy of Ioli Giomi.
135. Courtesy of Julia Santini.
136. Maryland Historical Society.
137. From *Columbus Revista* magazine (1924).
138. Lewis W. Hine Collection, Library of Congress.
139. Nebraska State Historical Society.
140. Immigration History Research Center, University of Minnesota.
141. Courtesy of Gary Mormino.
142. Courtesy of Carl Monastra.
143. Courtesy of Carlo Ferroni.
144. Temple University Urban Archives Center.
145. Courtesy of Anthony Scarpaci.
146. From *Columbus Revista* magazine (1920s).
147. Nebraska State Historical Society.
148. Eureka Federal Savings North Beach Museum, San Francisco.
149. From *Columbus Revista* magazine (1925).
150. Western Research Collection, Pueblo Library District.
151. Bain Collection, Library of Congress.
152. The Balch Institute.
153. Courtesy of Anthony Pizzo.
154. The Balch Institute.
155. Courtesy of Gary Mormino.
156. Courtesy of Carlo Ferroni.
157. Archives of Labor and Urban Affairs, Wayne State University.
158. Ibid.
159. Bain Collection, Library of Congress.
160. Ibid.
161. Utah State Historical Society.
162. Bain Collection, Library of Congress.

163. Archives of Labor and Urban Affairs, Wayne State University.
164. Ibid.
165. Immigration History Research Center, Bambace Papers, University of Minnesota.
166. Housing Association of Delaware Valley.
167. Library of Congress.
168. The Balch Institute, Italian Socialist Party Collection.
169. Ibid.
170. The Balch Institute.
171. Courtesy of Anthony Pizzo.
172. Bain Collection, Library of Congress.
173. Courtesy of Anthony Pizzo.
174. Di Leo Collection, Archives and Manuscripts Department, University of New Orleans.
175. Minnesota Historical Society, photo by P. Schawang, St. Paul.
176. From *Columbus Revista* magazine (no year given).
177. Special Collections, Photographs, University of Utah Library.
178. From *Columbus Revista* magazine (no year given).
179. Maryland Historical Society.
180. From *Columbus Revista* magazine (1925).
181. Di Leo Collection, Archives and Manuscripts Department, University of New Orleans.
182. Multicultural History Society of Ontario.
183. Di Leo Collection, Archives and Manuscripts Department, University of New Orleans.
184. The Balch Institute.
185. Chicago Historical Society.
186. U.S. Information Agency No. 208-FS-1780-2 in the National Archives.
187. U.S. Information Agency No. 208-FS-2119-1 in the National Archives.
188. Special Collections, Photographs, University of Utah Library.
189. U.S. Information Agency No. 208-FS-2591-2 in the National Archives.
190. Maryland Historical Society.
191. Courtesy of Anthony Pizzo.
192. Courtesy of Julia Santini.
193. Western Research Collection, Pueblo Library District.
194. Immigration History Research Center, University of Minnesota.
195. Multicultural History Society of Ontario.
196. Courtesy of Gary Mormino.
197. Courtesy of Carlo Ferroni.
198. Minnesota Historical Society.
199. Courtesy of Julia Santini.
200. Courtesy of Dante and Rose Fantasia.
201. Multicultural History Society of Ontario.
202. Courtesy of Dante and Rose Fantasia.
203. Minnesota Historical Society.

204. Utah State Historical Society.
205. Multicultural History Society of Ontario.
206. Western Research Collection, Pueblo Library District.
207. Courtesy of Joseph Dell'Alba.
208. Courtesy of Julia Santini.
209. Courtesy of Luciano Iorizzo.
210. Maryland Historical Society.
211. Minnesota Historical Society.
212. Courtesy of Anthony and Ann Sorrentino.
213. Western Research Collection, Pueblo Library District.
214. Courtesy of William D'Antonio.
215. Minnesota Historical Society, photo by P. Schawang.
216. Multicultural History Society of Ontario.
217. Minnesota Historical Society.
218. Maryland Historical Society.
219. Minnesota Historical Society.
220. U.S. Information Agency No. 208-FS-1259-2 in the National Archives.
221. New Jersey Historical Society.
222. Maryland Historical Society.
223. Courtesy of Gary Mormino.
224. Courtesy of Joseph and Vincenza Amato.
225. Maryland Historical Society.
226. Rhode Island Historical Society.
227. Multicultural History Society of Ontario.
228. Courtesy of Zena Valenziano.
229. From *Almanaco Italo Svizzero Americana* (1881); The Balch Institute.
230. Western Reserve Historical Society.
231. Eureka Federal Savings North Beach Museum, San Francisco.
232. Courtesy of Anthony Pizzo.
233. Courtesy of Rachel Becchetti Verretto and Helen Becchetti Dover.
234. Courtesy of Arturo Mazziotti.
235. Arizona Historical Foundation, Hayden Library, Arizona State University.
236. Western History Collections, University of Oklahoma Library.
237. Eureka Federal Savings North Beach Museum, San Francisco.
238. Special Collections, Photographs, University of Utah Library.
239. Multicultural History Society of Ontario.
240. Courtesy of Anthony Pizzo.
241. Courtesy of Luciano Iorizzo.
242. The Balch Institute, Covello Collection.
243. Maryland Historical Society.
244. Ibid.
245. Courtesy of Judge Gerald Sbarbaro.
246. Utah State Historical Society.
247. Di Leo Collection, Archives and Manuscripts Department, University of New Orleans.

248. The Balch Institute, Covello Collection.
249. From *Italian Tribune News,* Ace Alagna, publisher.
250. The Balch Institute, Covello Collection.
251. Ibid.
252. *Italian Tribune News,* Ace Alagna, publisher.
253. Ibid.
254. Ibid.
255. Ibid.
256. Ibid.
257. Ibid.
258. Ibid.
259. Ibid.
260. Ibid.
261. Ibid.
262. Ibid.
263. Metropolitan Opera Archives.
264. *Italian Tribune News,* Ace Alagna, publisher.
265. Ibid.
266. Ibid.
267. Ibid.
268. Ibid.
269. Ibid.
270. Ibid.
271. Ibid.
272. Ibid.
273. Ibid.
274. Ibid.
275. Magnum Photo, Inc. Photographer: Constantine Manos.
276. Courtesy of Mrs. Marie Di Nubile.
277. Magnum Photo, Inc. Photographer: Charles Gatewood.
278. Courtesy of Anthony Pizzo.
279. Multicultural History Society of Ontario.
280. Courtesy of Philip Cosentino.
281. Ibid.
282. Courtesy of Gary Mormino.
283. Courtesy of Pete "Figo" Carvella.
284. Courtesy of Catherine Gentile Scuderi.
285. Magnum Photo, Inc. Photographer: Elliott Erwitt.
286. Frederic Lewis, Inc., American Stock Photos.
287. Frederic Lewis, Inc. Photographer: Lawrence D. Thornton.
288. Courtesy of the Gerardi Family.
289. Courtesy of Jo Ann Pilardi Fuchs.
290. Multicultural History Society of Ontario.
291. Columbus Day Celebration, Inc., San Francisco.
292. Magnum Photo, Inc. Photographer: Bruce Davidson.
293. Magnum Photo, Inc. Photographer: Dennis Stock.

INDEX

The numbered references in this index refer either to textual material, which is designated by page numbers in lightface, or to caption material, which is designated by illustration numbers in boldface.